AMERICA ATTACKS JAPAN

AMERICA ATTACKS JAPAN

The Invasion That Never Was

TIM MAGA

THE UNIVERSITY PRESS OF KENTUCKY

Publication of this volume was made possible in part
by a grant from the National Endowment for the Humanities.

Scholarly publisher for the Commonwealth,
serving Bellarmine University, Berea College, Centre
College of Kentucky, Eastern Kentucky University,
The Filson Historical Society, Georgetown College,
Kentucky Historical Society, Kentucky State University,
Morehead State University, Murray State University,
Northern Kentucky University, Transylvania University,
University of Kentucky, University of Louisville,
and Western Kentucky University.

Editorial and Sales Offices: The University Press of Kentucky
663 South Limestone Street, Lexington, Kentucky 40508–4008

06 05 04 03 02   5 4 3 2 1

Frontispiece: Following the Japanese surrender, Mt. Fuji and part
of what might have been the U.S. invasion fleet is photographed
from the deck of the USS *South Dakota.* (Courtesy of the National
Archives Still Pictures Branch)

Library of Congress Cataloging-in-Publication Data

Maga, Timothy P., 1952-
  America attacks Japan : the invasion that never was / Tim Maga.
     p. cm.
  Includes bibliographical references and index.
  ISBN 0-8131-2248-1 (alk. paper)
     1. World War, 1939-1945—Japan. 2. World War, 1939-1945—
United States. 3. Imaginary histories. I. Title.
  D767.2 .M235 2002
  940.54'0952—dc21   2001007228

This book is printed on acid-free recycled paper meeting
the requirements of the American National Standard
for Permanence of Paper for Printed Library Materials.

Manufactured in the United States of America

To Kenneth Maga and Company C,
First Battalion, Third Marine Division

Contents

and bring life to that newly available documentation. And third, these sources provide amazing revelations that were never known or considered before in the few previous writings on this topic.

The invasion story is a human story. Real people were involved, not just memos and charts. Sadly, in the rush to describe a strategy or two, too many historians forget that fact. This is not just a tale of Plan A versus Plan B, or the proposed location for Division A on Landing Beach B. It is not a tale to cure the insomnia problems of the "greatest generation." This was a life and death struggle involving millions. It was the struggle of one people versus another, and many who lived through it deserve to be heard before it's too late. Hence, their memories are welcome in *America Attacks Japan,* and without apology.

This book is not the final word on the invasion story, and it never pretends to be a definitive study. It sheds light on an important event, and urges both writers and readers to consider the importance of "what might have been." Writing what could be labeled a "what if" story is considered an awkward thing in the historical profession. Yet history is filled with "what if" propositions. From "what if John Kennedy had lived" to "what if Hitler had taken England" are intriguing questions to general readers, but considered "pseudo history" to dyed-in-the-wool historians. On the other hand, some novelists and even filmmakers have asked and profited from trying to answer these kinds of questions. But considering the Japan invasion "pseudo history" has been a mistake, and the reasons are obvious. An American invasion was truly set for the fall of 1945, and Japan's defensive plan was in place as well. There was nothing "pseudo" about it.

As an American-born academic historian who lived many years in Japan, I heard both sides of the invasion story. Tall tales abound on both sides of the Pacific about what was planned or not planned. For instance, the image of the unswerving, fanatical Japan ready to commit mass suicide at the very sight of the American invaders is nonsense. And the image of Harry Truman's White House as 100 percent committed to nothing but unconditional surrender is in the same tall tale category.

But propaganda dies hard. Consequently, this book also separates the facts from the fiction, and takes into account Japanese plans and views as much as American ones.

In July 1945, the A-bomb decision changed everything, and *America Attacks Japan* explains why. Examining the morality (or lack of it) behind the A-bomb decision has become an entire field of its own. Again, this book never suggests to be the last word in such a debate, but it does make it clear where the invasion fits into it and how the invasion and A-bomb decisions are closely linked.

Trying to tell "the rest of the story" of the Japan invasion, as veteran news commentator Paul Harvey might say, is a mammoth undertaking. There are literally miles of archival documentation on the subject, and it is easy to see how historians can become overwhelmed by the topic or bogged down in minutiae. I owe a huge debt of gratitude to dozens of archivists for helping me climb this Everest of paperwork, and I hope that they will accept my general thanks here. But I do reserve special thanks to Randy Sowell at the National Archives–administered Harry S. Truman Library in Independence, Missouri, James Zobell at the Douglas MacArthur Memorial Archives in Norfolk, Virginia, Sam Anthony at the National Archives in Washington, D.C., and Hiro Kurashina at the Micronesian Area Research Center (MARC) at the University of Guam in Mangilao, U.S. Territory of Guam. Their help, leads, and documentation assistance were always welcomed. Finally, I would like to thank Douglas J. MacEachin, former Deputy Director for Intelligence at the Central Intelligence Agency and a Japan invasion expert, for his kind assistance to my wife and me during this project.

The invasion of Japan did not happen, but its significance to World War II must not be ignored or forgotten. The following explains why.

An official U.S. Army poster of a Superfortress bomber in the spring of 1945. (Courtesy of the National Archives Still Picture Branch)

camp. The American air raid began when the Kamatas were still in embrace, enjoying their happy reunion. Tomoko remembered being annoyed and frustrated by the bad timing of the raid, but her family believed that they had plenty of time to reach the nearby shelter after the first warning sounded. But civil defense warnings had become less and less reliable by April 1945, and the American air raids had intensified. Besides, it appeared that the Americans were more interested in the port facilities than the crowded downtown. The Kamatas were mistaken. The mixture of bombs and incendiaries danced their way to the displaced persons camp, and the Kamatas were forced to dash to the shelter. The elder Kamatas were too infirm to run, and Tomoko's mother, suffering from a fever, had little energy as well. But making it to the shelter also would have been a mistake. It was destroyed in the raid, and little Tomoko saw more of death that night than she would ever see again.

Tomoko's mother recovered from the burns, but the grief and depression never seemed to let go. Two years earlier, her husband had been reported missing in action and presumed dead somewhere in New Guinea. She had suffered so much, and then less than three months after the death of her parents Japan was on the verge of defeat. Life had lost all meaning to her.

There were thousands of Mrs. Kamatas across Japan, and years later Tomoko Kamata reasoned that her own mother's attitude about the war's end, like that of so many others at the time, was more attached to her own personal hell than to patriotic duty and responsibility.[2] Tomoko's mother favored the suicide of her entire family. This was more honorable, she said, than life in a "prison" administered by the killers of her loved ones. Such a death, she insisted, was the best response for all families soon facing national defeat and disgrace. The local government of the nearby small town of Zushi agreed.

In July 1945, the city fathers of Zushi formed the Ikego Defense League. Its administrators were war widows, and Mrs. Kamata was one of them. Their primary role was bomb and booby trap-making. Anticipating an American or Allied invasion at any moment, the League especially worried about the fate of their youngest children. Teenagers and adults could resist the invader and die a glorious death defending the homeland, but the children were a different matter. Most of the bombs and booby traps that Mrs. Kamata made day after day were meant to kill the children. These explosives looked like small ceramic pots, and they were tiny enough for a preschooler to handle. Plain or adorned with children's drawings, the pots were lined with gunpowder. A crude detonator was located near its mouth. Zushi and Ikego area children were expected to offer unsuspecting American GIs these particular gifts, and then trigger the detonator as they were accepted. Both the child and the American invader would be killed together. That was the plan,

hedonism, yuppies, and self-absorption ruled. After years of struggle and hard work, Japan saw itself as number one in the world economy. Looking back at the bad old days invited unnecessary and unwelcome arguments.[7] Ten years later, the Bubble had burst, and for the first time in years economic struggle was the rule rather than the exception. With the dramatic downturn in financial fortunes came a reassessment of the past, further stimulated by the fiftieth anniversary of the end of the Great Pacific War. After years of silence, public discussion of Japan's wartime role, the atrocities committed, and the postwar war crimes trials was now quite open and detailed. But a national consensus on World War II matters, including a sincere government-expressed apology to Asian/Pacific neighbors for the brutal Japanese occupation, was a far different matter. Yet the war discussion was a healthy one, permitting Japan to study both its past and its options for the future. When it came to the past, most discussants were concerned about how their country entered and fought World War II rather than how it surrendered. The issue of national suicide in the face of a probable invasion of Allied ground troops rarely entered that discussion.[8] Since the general debate was an amazing development in itself, talking about what truly happened in the bad old days was always more important than what might have happened. That gave little solace to people like Tomoko Kamata.

To Ms. Kamata, the "what might have happened" issue was the most important detail in the entire discussion.[9] National suicide, or at least her death and the death of her friends and relatives, had once been encouraged by government officials. Why, she asked? What had the Americans originally planned to do in their invasion, and did that plan stand in contrast to the post-A-bomb, post-surrender occupation government established by the "American Caesar," General Douglas MacArthur? Why, indeed, was she still alive, and what finally led her mother, and other mothers, to keep those ceramic pots in the cave? These were tough questions that went beyond the type of work most analysts were doing at the time. If at all, historians, military specialists, and interested journalists examined only the details of the individual code-named plans associated with the Allied decision to invade Japan. But, as Ms. Kamata suggested, there was more to the tale than the merits of Plan A versus Plan B, and she always worried that the answers to the tough questions would never be satisfying. Both a logistical and moral nightmare, the invasion plan had been extremely complex.

The Allies had talked about invasion for a long time. As early as 1942, President Franklin Roosevelt and his top military and civilian advisors decided that a vindictive, emotional response was not the way to write the peace with Japan. What was needed was a logical, level-headed assessment of the Pacific War.[10] Although victory at the time seemed especially elusive, White House planning for the invasion and final defeat of Japan began shortly after the fall of the Philippines in the spring of 1942. Despite this fact, even today's historical literature on the invasion topic is limited. In the face of the great moral debate over the appropriate or inappropriate use of the atomic bombs over Hiroshima and Nagasaki, few historians have cared about the "what might have happened" story. Those who have cared, such as John Ray Skates in his 1994 study, *The Invasion of Japan,* or Thomas Allen and Norman Polmar's 1995 work, *Codename Downfall,* have emphasized the lack of cooperation between the U.S. Army and Navy in the invasion planning. They also explain that the Allies overestimated Japan's home defense and wildly inflated their potential invasion losses. Preparing for the worst is one thing, these fine military studies suggest, extremism is another.

The Americans had faced a fanatical enemy, particularly during the ending months of the Pacific islands campaign. They expected even more fanaticism to meet their invasion of Japan. This reality influenced every step of their planning, injecting an element of fear and dread into their work that was not apparent in earlier military operations. In hindsight, that element or emotion makes both the planners and their plans look quite confused and struggling, and therefore easy fodder for today's World War II buffs to criticize or second-guess. With due respect to

suasion. In these heady days of finding the best invasion plan, and with the least casualties, McColm's ho-hum military rank did not diminish his important role.

With his new commission as a lowly lieutenant (jg) in the U.S. Navy, McColm still became the chief of agriculture on the Joint Army-Navy Invasion/Occupation Planning and Training Staff at the Presidio in Monterey, California. Without the uniform, he doubted that such a responsible position could have been possible, but, frankly, in less desperate times the role would have been exclusively reserved for an admiral or general. The Presidio housed the top secret project responsible for Japan

From left to right: General Douglas MacArthur, President Franklin Roosevelt, and Admiral Chester Nimitz meet in Hawaii to plan the final victory over Japan, July 26, 1944. (Courtesy of the FDR Library)

invasion planning, and McColm soon found himself involved in more than just discussions of agricultural matters.

McColm enjoyed the political significance of his new role. He maneuvered himself into policy discussions and decisions well beyond the scope of his original orders. His contributions to these discussions were often long and winded, but he would be rewarded for his commitment and interest with further administrative planning tasks. Ideally, and given the importance of the mission, Admiral Nimitz and General MacArthur, the senior invasion planners, were supposed to be leading most of these discussions, analyzing the twists and turns of every recommendation, and making the tough decisions. With the war still in full swing, Nimitz's and MacArthur's involvement in precise, day-to-day planning was limited. Be it 1945 or today, labeling a planning effort a Nimitz or MacArthur plan is too easily done. It ignores the many who labored day and night on the mechanics of one of history's greatest invasions. This was, indeed, something of the staff operation, although making that final decision was the toughest job of all.[17]

During the early weeks of 1945, McColm's Ten-Point Plan to invade Japan was accepted as the Presidio's "U.S. basic policy for the invasion and occupation of Japan." A mixture of U.S. self-interest, postwar vision, and guesswork, the "basic policy" represented something of a mission statement for the planners. The latter included dozens of little-known federal government bureaucrats, ambitious and not-so-ambitious military officers, along with a few famous figures, such as the prewar U.S. ambassador to Japan, Joseph Grew, and former Vice President Henry Wallace. General MacArthur and Admiral Nimitz were technically in charge of these early discussions, but in fact had no role in the writing of the mission statement.

The Ten-Point Plan was quite impressive. Implementing it was a different story. Point 1 called for American and Allied attacks on military targets only. According to McColm and his colleagues, the stepped-up and heavy bombing raids over Japanese cities in the early days of 1945 had killed too many inno-

ity, vengeance, and the relentless pursuit of total victory.[20] McColm believed that this type of emotionalism was influenced by wartime electioneering and racist propaganda. But the invasion planning was secret. There was no need, McColm noted, "to play to a crowd" because the crowd was not there. Because of that fact, he predicted that emotionalism would never rule the final plan. This observation was not a unique one. Roosevelt believed the same thing.[21]

Roosevelt and McColm were right. In contrast to their public statements, the politicos and military figures involved in the invasion planning process had more important things to do than denounce the enemy. Although the planners were always concerned about how they would look in the history books, they agreed that their best work was done in top secrecy.[22] If left to Congress or any open public policy decision, the invasion/occupation of Japan, McColm reasoned, would have resulted in the complete, irretrievable destruction of the entire country.[23] Consequently, McColm and his fellow planners saw themselves as above the emotionalism of the masses. In their own eyes, they were calm, collected, thoughtful men dedicated to doing the right thing. They also served a president whom some of them, like McColm, absolutely adored. The planners remained hopeful, rather than wildly optimistic, and always viewed their separation from public demands and concerns as the first ticket to success: "At the start of the invasion of Japan, we could expect to find 50% of the able bodied people in Japan out of work and hungry. The problem would be law and order. The Japanese government would provide the police protection for their people and also the occupying forces. The United States would use food rather than troops to keep the peace. The plan worked, secrecy triumphed."[24]

Often, McColm and his colleagues blurred the distinctions between invasion and occupation preparations. Considering the life-and-death importance of this work, one could logically assume today that the planning effort must have involved precise, detailed, and coordinated discussions. But this was rarely the case. The planners spent hours talking about "invasion strategy" when, usually, they meant "occupation duties." Or sometimes just the reverse. In a generic sense, the planners considered all of their work under the heading of invasion strategy. Years later, this appears quite confusing to anyone reviewing the official documentation of the planners. More to the point, the planners themselves were often at odds over proper direction and priorities.[25] Hot Springs proved it.

In January 1945, when the original Big Three (Roosevelt, Churchill, and Stalin) met in Yalta to discuss the coming end of the war (and a possible continuation of cooperation afterward), some of the Allied world's leading Japan experts gathered in Hot Springs, Virginia, to offer advice and guidance to the invasion planners. President Roosevelt had asked for this gathering, for many of the invasion planners knew little or nothing about Japan. According to General MacArthur, Roosevelt planned to act on many of Hot Springs' conclusions, but, as is the case in so much of the invasion story, it remains difficult to tell what Roosevelt might have done had he lived to see the summer of 1945.

At Hot Springs, the Japan experts were expected to wow the invasion planners with their wisdom, as well as report back to the Big Three on the general status of Allied planning cooperation in the upcoming invasion. The military specifics, such as what division lands on what beach, was not a matter of concern here. Basic objectives and goals remained the stress in Hot Springs. The experts talked, and the planners listened. Naturally, the experts, or advisees, as they preferred to be called at this meeting, saw their mission in an important light. They were helping Nimitz, MacArthur, and the others lay the political, economic, and diplomatic foundation for the invasion and occupation. Roosevelt had assured the American advisees that their conclusions, at the least, would be welcomed by the Allied heads of state.[26] Events were moving quickly, and there was a sense of urgency at Hot Springs. The U.S. invasion of Okinawa and the Ryukyu Islands was only weeks away. Although the Ryukyuan islanders had until the Japanese takeover seventy years earlier considered themselves a unique and independent culture from

important to them all. The American response to World War II had been an overwhelmingly positive and supportive one so far, Waymack reminded everyone, but those days were numbered.[1]

Waymack's pessimism was not met with universal approval. Dr. Chiang Mon-Lin, chairman of the Chinese advisees, responded quickly and angrily to the American's opening remarks. Calling Waymack a "reconstructed isolationist," "divisionist," and as Eurocentric as those he criticized, Chiang had little use for Waymack's warnings. He particularly wanted to know why the American believed the invasion would last two full years. Waymack seemed quite certain about it, and Chiang thought this prediction smacked of defeatism. Defending himself against Chiang's hurling of epithets, Waymack insisted that all he had intended to do was inform the invasion planners about deadly problems ahead. It was not, he said, his final word on the invasion, and considering Waymack's ability to speak-at-length on any topic, this was one of the grand understatements of the Hot Springs meeting. Consequently, he added a footnote to his opening remarks. Given the great heroism of the Nisei troops in Europe, he recommended that they soon be transferred to the Pacific, that more Nisei divisions be raised, and that all of them be landed as the first wave of the invasion. The Japanese, once the great champions of "Asia for Asians" and anti-Western racism, would be most confused by the courageous Nisei troops, he said. Meanwhile, the American people would be most impressed and further consider the importance of helping fellow American citizens, the Nisei, finish the good fight.[2] Chiang was not moved by this suggestion, but the planners would later incorporate Waymack's proposal in their final work.

"Nothing short of a total and complete defeat of Japan will guarantee us in the Pacific the minimum condition of peace."[3] With this comment, Chiang reflected the official position of his government. America must maintain its commitment to Japan's unconditional surrender, he said, for a postwar America would never be trusted in the Asian/Pacific region if some special arrangement, made out of invasion-related exhaustion, was made with Japanese politicians. He also thought the planners were spending too much time worrying over the creation of a post-invasion government in Japan. It clouded the immediate objective of a successful military assault on Japan. Allied assistance in the creation of a working, thriving Chinese democracy after the war, Chiang interjected, should be a higher priority than Japan's postwar recovery. He resented the fact that the planners' ten-point invasion/occupation mission statement seemed so generous to a brutal enemy.[4]

Although Hot Springs was characterized by its hot arguments, the meeting remained on track. It also remained dedicated to its heavily political agenda, and avoided detailed military matters. The advisees were academics, ex-diplomats, and successful businessmen. Some of them had at least served in the military and worked with the senior officer corps in the militaries of several Allied countries, but none of them were military strategists or tactical experts. At this early stage of the planning operation, directions and objectives had yet to be fully defined. Hot Springs was important to the process, although the meeting's ability to ignore or avoid precise military goals during an invasion discussion was a remarkable achievement. Agreeing on the big picture was required first, they believed, and even that would be easier said than done. Roosevelt had left the door open, suggesting that whatever happened at Hot Springs would make a difference in Allied policy-making.

Paul Emile Naggiar, chairman of the French advisee group, thanked the American president for trusting their judgment, but then went on to prove how argumentative that judgment could be.[5] If Waymack was right, and the Allied invasion continued for many months, the French government, Naggiar admitted, could not assist the effort. It had had barely enough arms and ammunition, he noted, to win the war at home against the Nazi occupation. Reminding both the advisees and planners that France had fought a difficult guerilla war of resistance against the Nazis, Naggiar predicted that fanatical Japanese troops and their civilian supporters might soon be "the French Resistance of Japan." Mission statement or not, if the Allied invasion became especially destructive, the occupation forces could "bank on guerilla activity," he said. Given his country's war torn condition, the requirements of its far-flung colonies, and the general war weariness of its people, Naggiar said the invasion planners should consider the fact that "an Allied reserve of troops," should the battle go bad, might not be there.[6] He meant a French reserve, but the point was well taken. Naggiar tempered this statement by insisting that France was ready to contribute to the invasion, but apparently this careful French diplomat was referring to moral support alone. Naggiar's comments tended to confirm what most everyone already knew. The Japan invasion and occupation was Allied in name and little else. The bulk of the effort would remain with the Americans.

It was the great Allied leadership conferences of World War II, and not Hot Springs, which represented good decision-making. The Big Three, sometimes preceded by specific ministerial and military meetings, had gathered in interesting places ranging from Quebec to Casablanca to Tehran. Real diplomatic and military arrangements had been concluded there, wedding the Allies to a policy, announced at the 1943 Casablanca conference, of unconditional surrender for the Axis powers. But at Hot Springs and in the general Japan invasion planning, the planners and advisees saw innovation and commitment paramount to existing diplomatic arrangements. It was up to the Big Three, they reasoned, to follow their lead and not the other way around. This view and approach was clear, obvious, and loudly expressed throughout the Hot Springs discussions. Defeating Japan, Chairman Tarr noted, was more important than conforming to any "aging diplomatic concern."[7] Although the Roosevelt administration and the Allied government leaders might have especially questioned the arrogant tenor and tone of this conclusion, Tarr was applauded by his colleagues for it. There was, at least, no disagreement that their mission was of a higher order than most matters of state at the time.

Sir Andrew McFadyean, leader of the British advisees and

the most eloquent politico in Hot Springs, was especially concerned where their higher order mission might lead. He urged caution in the effort to set policy, observing that the Big Three "might not be as easy to preach to" as expected. Policy-making by nature, he reminded his colleagues, is complex. Britain, for instance, he noted candidly, remained in great financial pain. London's postwar reconstruction alone would cost millions of dollars, and he could not guarantee that his and Churchill's political party, the Conservatives, would survive the argument over paying for it. More to the point, McFadyean worried that his country's domestic politics would interfere with the commitment to fight a long war in Japan. As early as 1942, Churchill had maintained the view that Britain must stand side-by-side with the Americans, through every step of the Japan invasion. Japan's defeat of the British Empire in Asia had been just as humiliating as the attack at Pearl Harbor. McFadyean echoed Churchill, noting that the "British people will not relax their efforts and consider the war with Japan as secondary." But the passion for war had faded in certain circles in England, he also admitted, and there were many who wanted reconstruction now and not later. In other circles, or to those obsessed with the effort to retrieve Britain's Asian/Pacific Empire, anti-Japanese hatred ruled the day. There was no doubt about it, he said. The domestic political battle between the Britain First advocates and the old line imperialists would affect the level of British participation in the Japan invasion.[8] This battle would continue regardless of who won the upcoming British election, and in January 1945 Churchill enjoyed no guarantees of returning to 10 Downing Street.

McFadyean's candor took the advisees and planners by surprise, and most interpreted his comments to mean that there was a wide gap between Britain's commitment to the invasion versus its actual and lasting participation in it. He did little to squash this concern. "Our vision is blurred and our nerves are frayed," McFadyean said of his country's political dilemmas. On the other hand, Britain would still try to maintain its commitments, he vowed, denouncing all those who suggested that his countrymen had completely lost their will to fight the good fight. Yet his sudden defense of British patriotism and resolve remained half-hearted and contradictory. This prompted Chairman Tarr to ask McFadyean a straightforward question. Would Britain fight on to total victory over Japan, particularly if the two-year bloodbath became reality? The British delegation leader had no comment.[9]

Mrs. V.L. Pandit, leader of the India advisees group, was especially disturbed by McFadyean's performance. To Mrs. Pandit, the real mission statement for the Japan invasion had yet to be addressed. The 1941 Atlantic Charter, whereby America and Britain agreed to champion self-determination and the benefits of democracy on a global scale, needed reaffirmation, she said. Good people everywhere, she believed, would be happy to support—even die for—the American and British campaign in Japan if these great democracies lived up to their noble rhetoric. Daringly, she suggested that America and Britain needed to demonstrate their commitment to postwar decolonization and peace. This was particularly important, for Japan had long touted its role as liberator of the European and American colonized Pacific. Why should India, or any Asian/Pacific colony, support a long, bloody invasion against "liberators"? Although she greatly agitated her non-Indian colleagues, Mrs. Pandit made it quite clear that she was not an agent of Japanese propaganda. Japan's Co-Prosperity Sphere, she admitted, had always been a smokescreen for a new Japanese Empire. But, the liberation propaganda had also been long in place, and Tokyo's commitment to it had been unswerving. America and Britain, she said, should be unswerving in the effort to enforce the Atlantic Charter. Only then would India and other nearby colonies be "happy to volunteer many troops" to the Japan invasion. Washington and London, the Indian advisee suggested, did not need to worry about a mediocre invasion force. "Millions were there," she said, if the Atlantic Charter truly represented the Allied cause. On the other hand, a Japan invasion based on Western revenge, would be viewed as another American and European assault on Asian/Pacific peoples. "No one will be there to help that cause," she warned, and the "plight of Japan" would win the sympathies of many in the Far East.[10]

McFadyean dismissed Pandit's concerns as the ravings of an Indian independence advocate. To Chairman Tarr, who expected to conclude a working agenda for the upcoming Japan invasion, no one could be dismissed. He thanked both McFadyean and Pandit for their clear observations, but it was also clear that difficult times were ahead. In contrast to the planning that characterized the Allied invasion of Europe only months before, there was a high, threatening, even dangerous political tone to the Japan invasion task. Finding an acceptable political arrangement that could keep the alliance together through its final battle with Japan was not going to be easy; however, President Roosevelt believed such an arrangement was essential to military success.[11] That belief, shared by most at Hot Springs, kept the advisee/planners meeting alive, relevant, and important. In short, the American president was aware of the political minefield ahead. The hot heads at Hot Springs offered a good preview of it all. Given the marriage of invasion and occupation planning, political and military arrangements were of equal importance to the White House. They always would be.

Urbano Zafra, chairman of the Philippines' advisee delegation, could agree with Roosevelt but disagreed with Mrs. Pandit's assessment of events. As an American colony, the Philippines, he pointed out, had every reason to be concerned about lingering U.S. or Allied colonial objectives. The independence of the Philippines from American rule had been guaranteed by the Roosevelt administration–supported Tydings-McDuffie Law of 1934. July 4, 1946, had been selected as the formal date for the transfer of sovereignty. The long war in Japan could delay or postpone that commitment, some in the Philippines might worry. Zafra was not one of them. America, he suggested in his own way, had the competence to walk and chew gum at the same time. In other words, it could win the war against Japan as well as keep its longstanding commitment to July 4, 1946. India, he pointed out to Mrs. Pandit, had not experienced the brutality of Japan's so-called liberation. He resented her cavalier discussion about Japanese policy objectives, for there was nothing cavalier about Japan's invasion of the Philippines. His country had suffered horribly during the Japanese occupation, fought hard against it, and wished America well in the coming fight in Japan. The Philippines, Zafra said, would be happy to volunteer troops to the effort, especially to help a living legend in the Philippines, Douglas MacArthur. They might not be in the first wave of the invasion, and their numbers would be small, but Filipinos would be ready to fight if needed, Zafra vowed, because it was the right thing to do.[12]

Advisee Zafra wanted no misunderstandings. The Philippines was grateful for its recent liberation from the Japanese occupation, and ready to contribute to the great battle ahead, but the July 4, 1946, commitment would have to be reaffirmed by President Roosevelt personally. Roosevelt responded as Zafra hoped he would, resulting in a blanket approval by the Philippines government of whatever invasion plan the Americans supported. Zafra's privately expressed thank you to the White House always remained in grand contrast to Pandit's conclusions, and, to a large degree, represented the type of warm, cooperative relationship Roosevelt hoped was possible with all the allies.[13] Had it been public, it might also have served as excellent Allied propaganda in its day: "The Leyte liberation has demonstrated to the world that the cooperation and collaboration of two peoples of two different races but of one human standard of relationship at its best, could be made a basis for understanding and solving some of the problems arising in the Pacific. . . . Here was a country which, forty-five years ago, was defeated, conquered and frustrated by the force of a mighty Power. But that Power has raised that country, helped and nurtured it, as a guardian cares for its ward. The same conqueror, now a benefactor, is ushering that same country into the family of nations. That is the picture today of American-Philippine relations in the Japan invasion."[14]

To the certain annoyance of the American advisees, the leaders of the Australian and Canadian advisee delegations offered comments more relevant to a graduate school seminar on world politics than to a hurried, dramatic summit of invasion experts. Most likely, this was because the chief Australian and Canadian advisors were both university professors. Professor Kevin H. Bailey for the Australians and Professor Edgar McInnis for the Canadians lectured their listeners on the troubles of British Dominions entering a new phase of the war. The group learned of Australia's anxiety over its economic isolation, along with its impatient desire for a special trade policy relationship with its former wartime partners. They also learned of Canada's exhaustion with World War II, its heavy loses so far in the war, and the belief that Canada could not make a real contribution to the Japan invasion. While Bailey implied that a long invasion would be unacceptable to Australia, McInnis suggested that Canada was too wounded to influence a short or long invasion. In their own winded way, both men stuck to these dismal assessments of their own nations' state of military health after many years of war.[15]

The long lecturing by the Canadians and the Australians prompted a British advisee, Sir Frederick Whyte, to criticize Chairman Tarr for his lack of control of the Hot Springs meeting. People were dying around the world, he pointed out, and time was running out. The "classroom discussions," he complained, were not producing a program of working Allied cooperation for the planners. It was time, he said, to address the specific issues, flesh out the McColm-designed mission statement, and get on with it. If anyone needed extra time to describe their plight, it was the Chinese, Whyte proclaimed—they had suffered more than Australia and Canada combined.[16]

Although Whyte's interruption might have been insulting to Australian and Canadian integrity, his point on the need to move ahead was well-taken. Hot Springs was always supposed to produce results, adding political and diplomatic significance to the precise military planning to come. But there was even disagreement over what the advisees and planners should call their fi-

of guerilla activity. This was technical stuff, in a way, but the Hot Springs delegates had no objection to wedding detail, now and then, to their larger mission of goals and objectives.

Immediate post-surrender measures also needed to be fleshed out. "Guerilla activity prevention," Chairman Tarr wrote President Roosevelt, might require some "outrageous" policy-making. His group, for instance, supported Allied assistance to Susumo Okano, leader of the Japanese Communist Party in exile in China, to subvert the abandoned Japanese army in China. To Tarr and his fellow experts, guerilla activity was a twin-headed dragon. It meant both bloody resistance in Japan and renegade commanders left in formerly Japanese-occupied countries carrying on the war as they saw fit. Korea, he noted, a place virtually enslaved by Japanese forces, could even serve as an industrial base of operations for these renegades for years to come. Even Emperor Hirohito, they worried, might retreat to Korea to lead, or at least represent, the renegade cause. They recommended a dramatic, new reaffirmation of the Allied leadership's pledge to anti-fascist resistance groups made at Cairo in 1943. More money, more men, as well as more under-ground operations (led by America's Office of Strategic Services) to link pro-Allied resistance and advancing Allied forces were required immediately, Tarr insisted. Together, the Allies and the long-suffering resistance movements in China and elsewhere could prevent the specter of "endless war on the continent."[20] As always, the precise means of doing this was never the concern of the advisees and the planners at Hot Springs. These were military matters, but, as often was the case, the political agenda of the Hot Springs group ran headlong into military decisions.

First of all, Chairman Tarr, concerned that war weariness might lead certain delegations to seek a separate peace with Japan, insisted on a Hot Springs Statement that reconfirmed Allied unity behind a Japan invasion. Since a Soviet delegation was not present in the Hot Springs meeting, such a statement was especially difficult to conclude. As a group, the advisees believed that any future Soviet role would be a minimal one.

They agreed that the noncommunist allies would be "well beyond the beaches" in the Japan invasion before any Soviet involvement became a matter of discussion. Tarr preferred that
Roosevelt "handle Stalin," for Soviet intentions in Japan would
be "based on the whim of the Russian dictator." Even Mrs. Pandit
of the Indian delegation worried that the Soviet Union represented "a new expanding totalitarianism." Like her advisee colleagues from other countries, she saw no invasion role for the
Soviets. Roosevelt would have to "mollify the Soviets in another
way." A long invasion, Pandit added, would encourage a Soviet
rescue and eventual Soviet domination of entire regions of Japan. Hence, she made distinctions between a hard and soft peace.
If Western colonial racism prevailed, she said, Japan would be
treated harshly in contrast to its ally, Germany. This hard peace
would haunt the victorious Allies for decades. Leniency would
assure the participation of Japanese liberals, she predicted, in
the post-invasion occupation government. This soft approach
to peace would also lessen the possibility of guerilla activity and
assure a united Japan in the face of Soviet imperialism.[21]

Thanks to Pandit's depiction of the Allies as racists, the Hot
Springs group was not averse to shouting matches and shot-
from-the-hip discussions that were barely relevant to the issues
at hand. Great Britain's Sir Andrew, for instance, reminded the
Hot Springs "ladies and gentlemen" that they were, indeed, "ladies and gentlemen." The best way out of a no-win argument
over racism and World War II was to end World War II, he proclaimed. With this challenge in mind, the Hot Springs group
wrote their recommendation for the terms of surrender. The
signatories, they insisted, must include the Japanese high command and the emperor himself. The latter's signature was viewed
as most important, for it would discredit the emperor's ability to
lead any post-surrender resistance. Although "morally" they
agreed that "Oriental peoples" (Asian/Pacific nations once oc-
cupied by Japan) should be the chief postwar administrators
over those who had oppressed them, only the United States
among the Allies had a sophisticated and involved history of

during the war years. Their very protest and involvement, according to this theory, would indicate an interest in democratic action. In the name of adhering to McColm's primary mission statement principle of maintaining "law and order," the advisees urged Allied occupation authorities to prevent violence and distribute what food they could find. On the other hand, they must still do nothing, the advisees insisted, to discourage the rise of popular movements. The democrats were in them, they said, and that was good for Japan. At that point, the emperor could be persuaded by the supreme allied commander to identify Japan's future with this rise of democracy. Consequently, the emperor, free from war crimes trials or any other Allied punishment, was needed to stay on. Representing past, present, and future, the emperor was the key to Japan's survival, said advisee Waymack of the American group.[25]

Truly complicating that survival would be the repatriation of thousands of Japanese troops from battlefields across the Asian/Pacific region. Because of it, the planners heard another heated debate among the advisees. The Filipino delegation, for instance, believed that not one single Allied ship should be wasted in an operation to transport Japanese POWs until Allied relief operations to remote Pacific islands and elsewhere were completed. The Australians, however, thought the Japanese POWs would be an excellent source, if necessary, of forced labor during the early reconstruction phase of the major Japanese cities. Nevertheless, few connected repatriation to forced labor. A cross-section of the advisees believed that the POWs would be so disillusioned with their former leaders that they would return home ready to build a new, exciting, and democratic government. But the Chinese delegation saw nothing exciting in an unruly mob that could "trigger horrible violence." The Americans especially countered this thesis, suggesting that specialists and technicians of all types were part of the returning armies. Today's soldiers could be tomorrow's nation builders, said the Americans, and they were needed for reconstruction work. These men did not, in the U.S. view, constitute the beginning of the end for Japan. The American position prevailed, as it would throughout the closing hours of the Hot Springs conference.[26]

Call it civil war, guerilla activity, unruly mobs, or angry POWs, if violence was to continue after the formal surrender of Japan, its perpetrators, the advisees unanimously agreed, must be forced to hunt for arms. All existing armaments, including armaments factories, the conscription system, and the secret police, would be eliminated as soon as the occupation government could accomplish it. Further disarmament measures divided the advisees. Once the threat of guerilla activity was over, argued the British and American delegations, a daring policy was required. They supported the creation of a new National or Home Guard in Japan. Dedicated to coastal defense and humanitarian relief work, this tiny version of the defunct Japanese Imperial Army and Navy would never be a threat to the Allies. But, it could be a source of continued national pride for Japanese citizenry. Eventually, it could move into more technological fields, such as radar, or even scientific research; however, it would remain divorced from regional or global responsibilities.[27]

The French, looking even further into the crystal ball, worried that a post-occupation, independent Japan would use this National Guard as a foundation for the resurrection of militarism perhaps as early as 1960. They demanded that Hot Springs support a post-surrender resolution against Japanese militarism. They also insisted on a formal commitment and announcement from the defeated Japanese, made to all the World War II allies, that their eventual, post-occupation independence would not lead to a new, large military. To the American delegation, all of this was so hypothetical and so far removed from early 1945 problems that the French demand made little sense. In any event, they agreed that the resurrection of Japanese militarism was wrong, and that any Japanese defense force must remain a small, inconsequential outfit for many years to come.[28]

To chief British advisee McFadyean, the French and his other Hot Springs colleagues were tackling the problem of a postwar Japanese military entirely in the wrong fashion. The French, he

more men to join that fight. Elsewhere, the threat of a long, ugly death by starvation could prompt the mass suicides that the invaders feared. If the invasion moved quickly and successfully, there would still be the problem of assisting rice farming areas that had been battlefields. The starvation threat would not end when the invasion ended.[34] McColm was expected to resolve all these problems before they happened. It was not an easy task, and he needed more cooperation from his superiors and the political community than existed in Hot Springs.

History, McColm learned, was not in the Allies' favor. Japan's large agricultural economy had been in trouble long before the war began. The trouble was rooted in tenant farming. In the twelve major agricultural prefectures, 60 percent of the cultivated land was worked by tenants. Absentee ownership of much of this land was great. In 1939 there were over 1 million individuals recorded as owning land who did not cultivate it themselves. The demand for land was so high that the few really large estates were never cultivated as a unit by the owners. They preferred to rent their holdings to tenants. Japan's largest farming estate, for example, included an area of over 4,000 acres divided among 2,500 tenants. More to the point, the numerous social and economic difficulties associated with tenancy had been at the root of Japanese political unrest for years. The tenants and some of the better-off groups of part-owners or part-tenants had provided leadership for Japanese extremist politics throughout that time. These same people would be in charge of feeding a country under siege, and they would also represent the leadership of the guerilla fighters, mass suicide movements, and/or the general resistance to the Allied presence in Japan.

This vanguard of extremist Japanese politics had a lot at stake, and their rise to power had been long and hard. After the abolition of feudalism in 1868, about 20 percent of the cultivated area had been tilled by tenants. The rapid adjustment from a feudal to a monetary economy worked hardship on many independent farmers. The necessity of obtaining cash to meet heavy taxation led many into indebtedness, frequently resulting in the loss of their land. The spread of tenancy was also facilitated by the fact that the landowners and well-to-do farmers, who owned more land than they could cultivate themselves, found it more profitable to rent to a multitude of tenants than to operate with hired labor. Moreover, for many years the Japanese middle class in the cities invested their savings in the purchase of land in accordance with the widely prevalent view that land was a gilt-edged security. The scarcity of land and insufficiency of alternative occupations bound the tenant to the land, regardless of the onerous conditions under which he worked. Rent contracts for a long period had been rare, although there was a so-called permanent tenancy system, adopted to facilitate the cultivation of newly reclaimed land. Most agreements had been oral, and for three- to five-year terms, but those involving fruit gardens ran from ten to fifteen years. Although tradition and custom suggested that an agreement could be changed or broken within a gentlemanly arrangement by both tenants and landlords, this was rarely the case. The landlord's domination of everyday life in the agricultural economy had been the source of bitter conflict between landlord and tenant, and the problem did not go away because of World War II. If the guerilla activity and mass suicide threats were quickly eliminated by the Allies, the victors would still inherit the confusion and social tension of the tenant farming situation. That meant additional challenges to keeping the country eating and healthy when the occupation began, and it also meant a lingering threat of further violence and unrest.[35]

Even the former Japanese minister of war, General Sadao Araki, had told the wartime Japanese press that food distribution would be difficult during the expected Allied invasion. Although terribly cryptic and cautious, Araki hinted that many would die not from Allied bullets but from starvation. Amazingly, he blamed history and his own government for not creating a more efficient agricultural economy over the years, one which the common man would have been happy to support. That creation, he implied, would have made the home defense "less worrisome" and more coordinated. "If we could have succeeded in solving the agrarian problem," Araki noted, "it would have been easier to solve the remaining serious social problems."[36]

McColm doubted that any decree from the Japanese militarist regime could have revamped their country's feudal-like agrarianism. Putting agriculture on a profitable basis might have been an important goal for Japanese government, but this concern had fallen far behind the incentives to create a booming armaments industry. Now, the latter was almost in ruins and Japanese farmland was soon to be a battlefield. An Allied landing in the early fall, McColm believed, was the best time to invade, for a food supply was at its height. Although safeguarding the large cities would probably be at the heart of Japan's defense, an Allied attack at a weak point, such as into the heavily agricultural communities of southern Japan or Kyushu, could bring the starvation, guerilla war, and suicide issues quickly to bare unless the Allies paid close attention to the progress of the Japanese harvest and moved swiftly away from the landing sites. As the Allies advanced to capture the cities, the immediate measures by the occupation authorities to remedy the old tenancy problem might be welcomed, McColm predicted, by the locals. Only a foreign presence would have the political competence and will to change the struggling agricultural situation, he argued. The larger goal here involved food distribution rather than winning the hearts and minds of troubled Japanese farmers. But the latter could result from the concentrated Allied effort to keep the agricultural economy moving while the invasion pushed forward.

Keeping the Japanese agricultural community away from extremist, anti-occupation government politics or violence required a grand plan before the Allies even hit the beach. McColm provided much of it. First of all, there was the issue of Japanese land hunger. The average farm was less than three acres. Assuming that Japan's cultivated area could be expanded by 3.5 to 4 million acres, as the last land survey in 1918 had indicated, it would make good economic sense for the occupation

authorities to declare the expansion upon arrival. The total cultivated land would increase from 15 to 19 million acres or 3.5
acres per farm household.

Second, even if the Japanese farm became a larger place to
live, it would still be too small to turn a healthy profit (according
to international comparisons). One Japanese farm usually looked
and worked the same as the next. A little American-like diver-
sity and innovation would go a long way, McColm believed, in
enhancing profits. Consequently, occupation officials would also
have to know something about farming, offering advice and assistance rather than the dictates and demands for conformity
that the farmers had endured for so long.

Third, the issue of tenancy needed to be addressed head on.
The efforts of the pre-militarist and wartime governments of
Japan to revise the system had failed. The Americans could
expect the same result. It simply had to go, and the farm work-
ers would become the owners of the land. Given the invasion-
wracked economy, McColm predicted most landlords would be
happy to sell off their holdings. The question then would be one
of price, and the ability of poor farmers to pay. A payment assistance plan sponsored by a generous occupation government
involving easy payments and long terms was the answer.

Larger farms, consolidation, and the end of tenancy would
also lead to less people working the land. But with the cities in
ruins and POWs returning home to unemployment, the issue of
potential unrest was still alive and well. Unskilled reconstruction work might contain the violence in the city; however, the
occupation government would also have to move quickly to shore
up its primary reforms in the rural areas. Scaling down indebtedness laws and procedures, lowering interest rates, levying
equitable taxation, cooperative marketing, and expert on-site
assistance, farm-to-farm, by occupation officials familiar with
the latest American agricultural advances were all required in
that shoring-up process. "Rural Reconstruction," McColm called
it, and it was not a term out of Roosevelt's New Deal vocabulary.
The term had been used by Japanese politicians in the 1930s to

describe rural reforms that never resulted. The Allies, McColm pointed out, would be providing those happy results, and the propaganda impact might be such that violent anti-occupation government activity would be swiftly rejected by "thinking Japanese." More to the point, the reputation for "evil" accorded to the Allies through years of Japanese propaganda would be proven incorrect.[37]

The challenge of the farming crisis in Japan had long been recognized by the Japanese political community, including former Japanese prime minister and army general Hideki Tojo. "How can the Army be indifferent to farmers' difficulties when it is largely composed of farmers' sons?" he once asked.[38] Inaccurately portrayed in American propaganda as the Japanese Adolf Hitler, Tojo had been prime minister at the time of the Pearl Harbor attack. The realization that "even Tojo," a hated symbol of tyranny in America, recognized the problems of rural Japan suggested to McColm and his superiors that the Allies must succeed where the enemy had failed.[39]

While McColm and his Rural Reconstruction colleagues shared the general fear of guerilla war and mass suicides to come, they also had great faith in their plan to address Japan's historic dichotomy of booming industrial centers and medieval agriculture. But they had to beat the expert prediction of a two-year campaign—only swift agrarian reforms by the occupation government could save the country from both starvation and behind-the-lines violence. Both MacArthur and Roosevelt were intrigued by the possibilities (as described to them by McColm). To McColm, a certain historic precedent was about to be set, and only technical questions remained in reference to its implementation: "The drastic agrarian changes in the countries of central and eastern Europe, following the military defeats in the First World War, furnish precedent that cannot be disregarded. Japan need be no exception. The real question, it would seem is rather of the character of the reform: Will it be a drastic one or will it proceed step-by-step and inch-by-inch? Will it be a spontaneous one or controlled and directed? Finally, who will pay for

From left to right: General Douglas MacArthur, President Franklin Roosevelt, Admiral William Leahy, and Admiral Chester Nimitz discuss the invasion of Japan, July 1944. (Courtesy of the National Archives Still Pictures Branch)

the cost of agricultural rehabilitation? No ready answer can be given to these questions, for much will depend upon the nature of the peace terms that the Allies will impose upon defeated Japan."[40]

McColm's immediate superior, for a time, was Major General John Hilldring. The Presidio-Monterey operation had been his idea. Hilldring also had been a leading force in the establishment of other "Specialty Schools for bureaucrats." These schools stressed Japan studies in history, economics, and other matters. A Japan invasion planner would attend these schools, located in Charlottesville, Virginia (Army) and Princeton, New Jersey (Navy), before being assigned to the Presidio. Having little

starvation/violent response problem once they reached Japan. There was little written work that he could use in his classroom. While working on his master's degree, Ladejinsky had written on the politics of Japanese agriculture, and McColm assigned it. He had never met Ladejinsky before the Presidio. He also had no idea he was assigning the writing of his soon-to-be replacement, the future agricultural reformer in Japan. McColm's concerns had remained invasion-focused. A long-term, postwar reform of the Japanese agricultural system had been part of that concern, but it would be a peacetime preoccupation of Ledejinsky and MacArthur.

Recognizing the significance of McColm's invasion date and location recommendations and Hilldring's support of them, the White House agreed that no invasion of Japan would take place while there were crops in the field.[44] McColm's report on food/agriculture-related priorities had been countersigned by over forty of his colleagues, and President Roosevelt had no reason to dispute them. Three points had been argued in defense of this decision, and all of them involved military strategy. First of all, MacArthur advocated landing 1400 tanks in the first wave of the assault. Japan was a rice-growing country with miles of flatland. With the rice crop in the field, water would be a problem both for the tanks and the foot soldiers marching behind them. Only the enemy would benefit from such a situation. Second, a good rice growing period was also associated with heavy rainfall. This only accentuated the water problem, making most of the many irrigation ditches and streams too deep to ford. Third, the air offensive over Japan during the opening hours of the invasion was expected to be quite successful. The significant bridges left undestroyed in previous air raids would not be left standing this time. Wide rivers separated many interior Japanese cities from the rice fields. Without bridges, those cities would become medieval-like fortresses, complete with wide, deep moats, distancing them from a water-logged invading army with their tanks already sinking in the mud. In short, as the exhausted Allied armies sloshed forward, they would be faced with yet another

water-related crisis. Even if some of the bridges remained standing, few of them, according to still-existing prewar Japanese con-
struction codes, could handle the weight of several American-made
tanks. A dry season attack remained essential to success.

The American Joint Chiefs of Staff favored an assault where
the invading armies could consolidate their strength quickly
and only then move forward into the heart of Japan. Rural southern Japan or Kyushu seemed to promise this early success, but
it also represented the water-logged nightmare detailed by the
Presidio group. On the other hand, if the military judged the
proper timing, Kyushu was still a good selection for the first
strike. Some of its rice was grown on what farmers call "benches,"
and thanks to the warmer weather in that part of Japan those
same farmers also grew barley in the winter. McColm's team
advocated an invasion to be timed with the plowing of the barley. If the Allies invaded too soon, the water problem would still
be there. If they invaded to late, they would destroy the barley
crop and contribute to the starvation-related problems the
Presidio had been tasked to prevent. McColm and his colleagues
set October 31 or November 1, 1945, as the best dates for the
attack, and the Joint Chiefs accepted the plan by July 4, 1945.
McColm and the Presidio would have no role in naming this
first strike, codenamed "Olympic," or the specific military decisions to follow. They had done their groundbreaking work, and
Washington welcomed it.[45]

In total, some nine hundred potential invasion/occupation
administrators and technicians were trained throughout the
Presidio's planning operation, or "Japan CASA" (Japan Civil Affairs Staging Area). Although many of these men were headstrong and ambitious, the arguments and disagreements over
policy had been more of a problem in Hot Springs and not
Monterey. There had been two serious arguments in the Presidio
group, and both were quickly resolved. One involved the policy-
making role of the so-called old Japan hands, namely former
ambassador to Japan Joseph Grew and his embassy staff. Grew
and his colleagues considered themselves the real authority in

3

The Early Peace Feeler

As late as the summer of 1945, and in spite of official statements to the contrary and signed agreements with the Allies, the White House entertained what George Elsey (administrative assistant to President Truman and special assistant in Pacific affairs) called "other avenues to unconditional surrender." Especially after Germany's May 1945 capitulation, key members of Congress and various VIPs from the press, academe, and the religious community began a certain offensive in favor of a "quick and humane" end to the war in the Pacific. President Harry Truman paid close attention to it during the days before the A-bomb decision and the final push against Japan.

Hitler's defeat brought jubilation to the White House, but ending the war in the Pacific raised questions and doubt. Later, at the time of the Japanese surrender, this period of soul-searching and confusion suddenly seemed sad and embarrassing to the Truman team. Long after the war, Truman administration figures would still be denying that these dark days of struggle ever took place. The more heroic image of unswerving determination and commitment was much more pleasing.

The secret American-Japanese contacts began in Europe during early May 1945, and the effort was spearheaded by Ishio Fujimura, the principal Japanese naval representative to the surrendering Nazi government. Following OSS confirmation that

Kitamura had learned of the Fujimura effort from Shunichi Kase, the Japanese minister to Switzerland, and the minister, said Kitamura, also supported the peace feeler. By July 1945, this effort to win Allied favor was touted by Fujimura, Kase, and Kitamura as a soon-to-be "grand success" when Brigadier General Kiyotomi Okamoto offered his full support to the effort. Okamoto was the former Japanese military attache in Switzerland who, in the late spring of 1945, had been dubbed chief of Japanese military intelligence in Europe by his superiors in Tokyo. Okamoto was believed to be in daily contact with the Japanese government, and although far from home he was still a powerful voice (at least in Army and pro-Army circles) within Japan's militarist regime. The OSS had been under the impression that only the Navy and a handful of civilian supporters were in favor of a quick deal with the Allies. Army generals, such as former Prime Minister Hideki Tojo, were viewed as spoilers in the OSS analysis, i.e. those who would thwart any effort to surrender too quickly. Okamoto tilted this analysis, suggesting that peace might be supported from a variety of quarters in the confused Japanese government.

Fujimura and his peace feeler colleagues were quite aware of the unflattering Allied view of their government. Okamoto's support meant that the Army was indeed "ready to deal," or so they told the OSS. Moreover, peace was possible "today," Kitamura said in mid-July 1945, and with only a "handful of Allied guarantees."[2]

On July 19, 1945, General Okamoto even wrote his government explaining that "the war was lost" and that the Switzerland peace feeler merits their immediate endorsement. There was no response, but Okamoto and his colleagues told Allen Dulles in Allied-occupied Wiesbaden, Germany, that this did not mean total rejection. Consulting his superior, OSS Director William Donovan, Dulles was not sure what to do next. There had been much talk and little action. Nicknamed "Wild Bill" by both his friends and political foes, Donovan always preferred action. In fact, he doubted that the Japanese peace feeler was anything more than a bizarre Switzerland-based phenomenon. He also saw little reason to depart from the unconditional surrender route. This did not mean America would close the doors to peace advocates, he told Dulles, although it was unclear what a cracked or fully open door might offer the Allied cause of fascist destruction and democratic enlightenment. Donovan was more candid with President Truman about the peace feeler: "I believe that for the next few days important developments in this matter are not likely, but that a line is being opened which the Japanese may use when the situation in Tokyo permits unconditional surrender."[3]

Besides the argument over whether unconditional surrender was truly the last word, or whether the peace feeler advocates could win Tokyo's full endorsement, there was another OSS concern. The peace feeler supporters presented a united front, but in reality they were as confused as the businessmen, royalists, Army generals, and Navy admirals who represented the government in Tokyo. General Okamoto, for instance, insisted on negotiations with the Americans alone. He hated the British and did not trust the Soviets. Hence, he urged his colleagues to quit talking about arrangements with the "Allies," and in his own communications with Tokyo he only mentioned a peace settlement with the Americans. Minister Kase disagreed with Okamoto as well as with the general thesis that communist revolution was around the corner in Japan. Capitalism was too deeply rooted there, he correctly pointed out. He also did not want Japan caught in the middle of a row between the Soviets and the Americans over the future of his country. With all these concerns in mind, he urged his colleagues to support a negotiation effort with the Soviets. This request sparked an intense argument in the small group, which also helped explain why the OSS–peace feeler talks dragged on for over two months.

Unable to reach an agreement with the Americans, and in despair over the fate of his country, General Okamoto committed ritual suicide in early August 1945. He left behind a lengthy suicide note, praising the peace feeler group as heroes who might have saved Japan from further war casualties. In respect for his years of service, the Japanese government eulogized Okamoto as a "champion of peace." More than a little desperate themselves, Fujimura and Kitamura interpreted this statement to mean a full endorsement of their efforts by the Tokyo regime. They urged the OSS to see it the same way, and to permit them a few days to set up the surrender terms. Nothing came of this particular matter. Meanwhile, there were other peace efforts underway, but the seriousness behind these efforts was another matter.

What amounts to the oddest peace feeler activity involved an American and not the Japanese. In fact, what Ellis Zacharias, the deputy director of the Office of U.S. Naval Intelligence, did or did not do remains a matter of speculation. Shortly after the war, Zacharias published accounts of Japan's early interest in peace and the plans to surrender months before the atomic bomb blasts. Zacharias's short articles always promised that larger book-length analyses were in the wings, and that all questions about his involvement in early 1945 negotiations with Japan would be answered there. The books were never written, and the questions remain.

Zacharias claimed that the U.S. effort to win the peace without invasion included a variety of negotiators in the field. They ranged from actor Douglas Fairbanks Jr. to the Pope, and their efforts involved, for instance, asking "Emperor Hirohito's peace-loving mother" to lobby her son and the government on behalf of "immediate surrender." They also asked Stalin to "scare the Japanese into surrender" via publicly announced threats of "total destruction" in an upcoming Soviet attack. Zacharias himself claimed that his own July 21, 1945, radio broadcast to Japan had an important impact on the end of the war. In this Japanese language broadcast, transmitted from the Office of War Information, Zacharias insisted that "the Atlantic Charter and the Cairo Declaration are the sources of American policy." This statement, he claimed, constituted a deliberate Truman administration ploy, whereby the Japanese would be informed that the United States was well-aware of Japan's desire to end the war, its wish to see the term "unconditional surrender" better defined by the Allies, and its fear of potential ruthlessness on the part of the upcoming occupation government. Besides claiming this important personal role in bringing the war to an end, Zacharias' postwar writings accused both the Roosevelt and Truman administrations of unnecessary warmongering and of prolonging hostilities.

To the Center for Japanese Studies at the University of Michigan, which investigated Zacharias's claims in an in-depth research effort of 1974, the Zacharias data and anti-Roosevelt/ Truman thesis were exaggerated and politically motivated. Indeed, when it came to "end of the war confusion," the Center saw Zacharias at the center of it. They questioned the seriousness of his office's negotiations effort and believed that the White House was more concerned with the possibility of hundreds of thousands of Japanese troops in China returning home to defend Japan against an Allied invasion than anything Zacharias was doing. Concern and various discussions did not equal serious negotiations or policy, the Center concluded. The Center's researchers urged historians to take a closer look at what did or did not happen with the OSS-Japan negotiations. Much of the material to answer the Center's questions was still classified in 1974, and their focus had been on the closing efforts of the Japanese peace feeler and not Zacharias's friendship with Douglas Fairbanks.

In that closing effort, Fujimura and Kitamura continued to stress the importance of Hirohito remaining on the throne, adding additional reasons why that must be the case. Those reasons involved the endeavor to win a complete surrender of Japanese troops trapped in China. Only the emperor could succeed in the effort, they insisted, echoing unwittingly a concern at America's Hot Springs conference. Dulles and Donovan continued to listen, but again offered no commitments. When the Japanese government did indeed surrender, Fujimura and Kitamura turned over a transcript record of all discussions held

lations and pondered the Allied occupation period as well. Judd wanted the Army generals and Navy admirals to leave Japanese government service, pending war crimes trials of their own, before the peace negotiations began. It made no sense, he argued "in the name of ethics and common sense," to wheel-and-deal with murderers. The best peace deal, he suggested, would come from arrangements made with the civilians in the Japanese government. These individuals were businessmen and "thinking people" concerned about the future and not the glorious past, he believed. Hence, they would work with the Allies to build a working peace deal. He had examples of what that workmanship might entail.

In Judd's opinion, the Japanese faced utter destruction. Those civilians who hoped to save Japan would have to promise the American negotiation team that the expunged military elements of their government would not soon return. Touting Japan's rigid, disciplined education system, Judd insisted that the Japanese civilians in government service had always been bright, intelligent men who knew how to make "good decisions." Consequently, the Americans should not press them, he said, on post-surrender issues. Most Americans, he assumed, would support a postwar Japan that purged itself of its pro-fascist past, taught its children to respect democracy, quickly adopted an American-like legal system, and went about the business of business. If the U.S. negotiation team, he worried, pronounced that Washington would be in full control of postwar Japan for awhile, those courted civilians in the Japanese government might declare their solidarity with Army and Navy nationalists. A generous Allied occupation policy, whereby the locals determined much of their own future, equaled the type of democratic cause championed by the Americans and their friends throughout World War II, Judd stressed. In short, the mechanics of the post-surrender government, he said, had to be presented to the Japanese during the negotiation process. American revenge, paternalism, and a strong-armed administration must be rejected before those negotiations begin, he pleaded, and he won applause from educators for it.[9]

To a large degree, Judd, like Lucas and McClellan, simply assumed that unconditional surrender was more propaganda than policy, and that the Truman administration would soon be ready to deal with Tokyo. Winning the emperor's abdication was seen as an easy process for any effective politician in Japan, particularly given the alternatives of war and misery. For this reason Judd could wax poetic on what the occupation government should look like. In fact, most of his speech-making stressed his vision of a happy postwar Japan side-by-side America in its stand against advancing communism. During July 1945, Judd even made the assumption that the president needed copies of these nation-wide speeches, and before meeting the Allied leaders at the Potsdam conference. He sent them to the White House just hours before Truman left for this European meeting, hoping they might have some relevance to the discussions on Japan. Truman thanked the Minnesota Congressmen for his efforts. He also asked his special assistant, George Elsey, to survey the public impact Judd was scoring over his particular point of view.[10] But events were moving too quickly, and no study was ever completed.

In spite of his "Give 'Em Hell Harry" image, Truman was also governed by old-fashioned Midwest manners and etiquette. He often formally thanked people for offering their views against him, such as Congressman Judd. But he never fired off a thank you to New York Governor Thomas Dewey for his views on Japan. Dewey, the defeated 1944 Republican presidential candidate, shared an assessment on Japan's surrender similar to Judd and the other doubters of the unconditional surrender approach. Also dreaming of a 1948 presidential bid, Dewey was much more cautious than members of Congress on Japan invasion-related issues. His position dated back to September 1944 at the height of what once seemed like a close challenge to Franklin Roosevelt's effort to win a fourth term. It also coincided with another Allied conference, in Quebec City. At that time, when asked by veteran *New York Times* reporter Warren Moscow about the unconditional surrender of Japan, Dewey had plenty to say about how the war in the Pacific must end.

Christianity and Crisis: A Bi-Weekly Journal of Christian Opinion, agreed with Niebuhr, along with his distinguished editorial staff (including Christian writers and Democratic Party activists Charles Burlingame and Henry Van Dusen, historian John MacKay, and multi-million dollar contributor to the Democratic Party and Eleanor Roosevelt confidant F. Ernest Johnson). These individuals and others, including New York luminary and socialite Rhoda McCulloch, sent Truman "A Statement on Our Policy Toward Japan" echoing Niebuhr's complaint against unconditional surrender "sloganism."[14]

The Japanese, they said in their statement, have no way out. Their cities are being obliterated (which Niebuhr and his colleagues also opposed), and they have no way of knowing if surrender will lead to more or less misery. Truman, in any event, had already addressed this matter of concern earlier in his presidency during a meeting with Niebuhr and Christian leaders. At that time he had told this religious delegation that the Allies had no intention of totally destroying Japan. He encouraged them to look at the bright side, promising to champion a healthy U.S.-Japan relationship within days after the surrender.[15]

By June 1945, Truman's assurances no longer had much meaning to the religious delegation. They demanded some immediate indication of America's plan for invasion and the follow-up occupation government. Insisting that they did not demand that the U.S. military reveal top secret matters which could harm Allied troops, Niebuhr and his colleagues explained that a little candor could go a long way. In short, if the Japanese had some idea of what might be in store for them, there also might be a better chance for a peace settlement. If the Japanese called for negotiations, they said, then the White House should honor their wishes.

Niebuhr also feared that racism guided military decisions toward Japan. The air war campaign of obliteration was much more severe in Japan than over Germany, he claimed. After Germany's surrender, General Dwight Eisenhower, the overall Allied commander in Europe, even told America's Federal Council of Churches that the destruction of European cities from the air might not have been a "military necessity." He also implied that this strategy would not be stressed in the Pacific. Niebuhr asked Truman for further clarification, urging him to halt the air campaign over Japan, open negotiations, and end the war. There was no real need to wait for the Japanese to make the first move, he said. For the moment, according to Niebuhr, the Japanese were too afraid to act. America, he said, could initiate and win the peace quickly. If the White House failed to make that initiative or rebuffed a Japanese peace offer, Niebuhr promised a vocal and determined campaign of "activism by fellow Christians" to force the Truman administration's hand: "We are concerned over the interpretation of the slogan, unconditional surrender. Surrender is a military act. The demand that it be unconditional in no way precludes a statement by our government in explicit terms of what the economic and political consequences of surrender for the Japanese people will be. The failure to make such a statement prompts the Japanese to delay an ultimately inevitable decision through fear of unnamed consequences. We believe that it is morally wrong and politically dangerous for any nation to ignore long-range considerations of policy by allowing military strategy alone to control its relations even with enemy nations."[16]

Given the priorities of state and wartime obligation, Truman might have ignored veiled threats of religious/political action against him. Wisely, he took the time to deal with the *Christianity and Crisis*–based complaint. This did not mean Niebuhr and his colleagues would win the answer they wanted, but the president did suggest that their views "now received careful consideration." Peace, he said, was his top concern. Without getting into any specifics, he also said that top secret invasion plans did not involve "obliteration," and that a "generous" postwar occupation was assured. William Hassett, the secretary to the president, helped Truman draft his careful words to Niebuhr and his friends. Obviously, those words would soon be public knowledge, and Truman had no objection to the Japanese also

In June 1945, President Harry Truman greets former President Herbert Hoover in the Oval Office of the White House. (Courtesy of the Harry Truman Library and Stock Montage)

troops out of harm's way during the 1931 Japanese invasion of Manchuria won him the reputation as a spokesperson not just for peace, but for "peace at any price." The latter, of course, was not a complimentary statement, and years later during World War II Hoover's 1929–1933 foreign policy suggested naivete and even irresponsible behavior to some.[2]

Although a Democratic Party loyalist, and proud of it, Harry Truman disagreed with the Hoover-bashers. He sympathized with the pressures Hoover had endured, admired his commitment to peace, and thought the poor man had received a hatchet job from the press and the Democrats. Truman also admitted to former Secretary of State Cordell Hull that he enjoyed "shaking up" reporters with his "unpopular views" on Hoover.[3] Consequently, in June 1945, when Hoover submitted his Japan peace plan to the White House, Truman studied it respectfully. He ordered Secretary of State Edward Stettinius and his staff to do the same. He then passed it on personally to ex-Secretary of State Cordell Hull for his views and gave it to Secretary of War Henry Stimson (also Hoover's former Secretary of State) for his analysis. Indeed, the report was taken quite seriously, and Truman would find plenty of policy recommendations in Hoover's grand analysis which he could support. He seemed pleased to be able to report that fact to his old friend, the ex-president.

Given the approaching collapse of the Japanese defense on Okinawa, Hoover believed that there was "a bare chance" of ending the war with Japan before July 1945. "Bare" or not, he advocated an immediate peace mission. For that mission to work, the United States would have to reassess its objectives, and he submitted several "talking points" for the Truman administration to consider.

First of all, Hoover admitted that the war "fundamentally arose over the Japanese invasion of Manchuria." That invasion, of course, took place during his watch, and logically he thought this initial "problem with Japan" needed to be addressed right from the start of the negotiations. Manchuria must be restored to Chinese rule, he said. Hoover believed that stressing this restoration as a primary interest of the Allies would also teach the Japanese about the importance and sanctity of international agreements. Their 1931 invasion had violated that sanctity, and their success in Manchuria had encouraged them to try it again. The days of Japanese sword rattling were now over, and the Tokyo regime must recognize that fact, Hoover said, from the

must be returned to China, along with other Japanese-occupied regions nearby. The Allies had already made that point in the 1943 Cairo Declaration (a carefully crafted statement on behalf of the aging democratic commitments to self-determination and decolonization). Reparations, most everyone agreed, equaled bad policy-making, but Hoover's labeling of Japanese property transfers back to China as reparations was, they noted, a clever suggestion. Meanwhile, an Allied-run post-surrender government in Japan had been in the planning stages for months. Japanese militarist participation in it, or in the postwar effort to rebuild Japanese business, was to be refused as noted in the Hoover plan. On the other hand, the group took exception to Hoover's token implication that a handful of symbolic war crimes trials might be good enough. They also rejected the idea that Japan should be in charge of most of its postwar future while the occupation government would do little or not even be necessary.

On the one hand, the Hoover report, the analysis group acknowledged, was not all bad. The ex-president's point on the "priorities of negotiation" versus postwar planning, for instance, was declared "thoughtful" by the group. On the other hand, they found little else in the thoughtful category. The State Department analysts were especially quick to point out that Hoover was too loose with American war aims. How could one be a champion of Manchurian integrity but condemn Korea and Formosa to more years of Japanese colonization? Most reports, both public and top secret, that the State Department received had told a tale of Japanese brutality in Korea and Formosa. In any event, the Cairo Declaration had been clear. Japanese colonization was supposed to end without exception, and the analysis group saw no reason to change that commitment. Hoover's faith in the Japanese government to do what was right, reject militarism, and move forward in harmony with its former enemies represented the height of utopian dreaming to the group.[11]

More to the point, although Hoover's proposal could be provocative at times, well-written most of the time, and passionate all the time, it did little, said its analysts, to induce the Japanese to surrender. Their final word was not very flattering to Mr. Hoover.

> It is our view, however, that a mere call on the Japanese to surrender, in whatever terms it might be couched but without clarification of unconditional surrender, is not likely to bring any affirmative response. We feel, on the other hand, that there might conceivably be a derisive rejoinder by the Japanese, with such effects on the morale of the American people as it might be difficult to predict. We have therefore prepared a draft statement which would, on the one hand, call upon the Japanese to surrender in terms substantially those proposed by the Joint Chiefs of Staff, and would, on the other hand, indicate to the Japanese those things which, after their surrender, we would intend to accomplish in Japan.[12]

Truman had little problem agreeing with the conclusions of the Hoover response group, although he commented pensively that he hoped "history is on our side."[13] He also admitted that he wished he understood what made the Japanese tick. Indeed, Truman's view of Japan was less sympathetic than Hoover's, and he knew little about the country. Truman even noted privately to his staff that he was "painfully ignorant" about Japan. Because of this fact, he had asked George Elsey to produce a specially written *Policy Manual on Japan* for him shortly after he became president in April 1945. Truman never became an authority on things Japanese, but his grasp of Japanese life and politics would improve as the months went by.[14]

During the spring and early summer of 1945, Truman's view of Japan was not that different from the propaganda-influenced American citizenry. What he did know came from a round-about way. While serving in the U.S. Senate, Truman had become something of an expert in the financing of World War II military operations in the Pacific. He had a solid, self-taught economic grasp of the war with Japan. Thanks to that knowledge, he was able to criticize both China's and New Zealand's misuse of Ameri-

president had been concerned that some of these brilliant young men, including his assistant naval aide and rising political star Clark Clifford would not return alive from the Japan invasion. That possibility truly disturbed Truman. He assured these staffers that the White House would "never erase the option for peace."[21] But what did this mean?

Pinning down the real Harry Truman on the unconditional surrender issue became a deep matter of concern to Philleo Nash, the special assistant to the director of the Office of War Information. If Truman was flipping and flopping, he wanted to know about it. The new president's comments to different White House personalities were supposed to have been in confidence, if not top secrecy. But word got around anyway. Nash was the propaganda workhorse behind most of War Information's efforts. He supported unconditional surrender and his office had been defending—if not touting—the unconditional surrender decision for months. The decision remained a "magnificent one," he told Truman, and he took it upon himself to explain why the president should continue to support it.

To Nash, there was no alternative to unconditional surrender. If the president was considering "some deal with the Japs," he pointed out, then U.S. security would forever be in jeopardy. Japan's full ability to wage aggressive war would be quickly restored once a "deal" was made, he insisted, and America would be fighting Japan throughout the next decade. Unconditional surrender would avoid this particular madness.

Nash said that he appreciated the president's concern over casualties, including those of the young men he admired in his own Oval Office. But, "we must be ready to do whatever is necessary in order to make it [the war's end] complete and final."[22] War Information had been hammering out this specific message for two years straight, and many Americans had volunteered to fight in a war that crushed fascism. It would be political disaster for the Democratic Party and the Truman White House, Nash predicted, if the president backed away from the unconditional surrender decision. Nash, a soon-to-be executive committee chairman of the Democratic Party of Wisconsin and a lieutenant governor there as well, was quite the political animal. He also believed that no one in the White House ever considered the domestic "political vitality" of the unconditional surrender decision. They should do so, he pointed out, for it held both "long-lasting security and political benefits." The party that defeated Japan, he reminded Truman, could be the truly dominant party for the rest of the century. The party "which dealt with Japan" faced a different fate.[23]

Nash did admit that the coming invasion of Japan also presented some political risks. Yes, the casualty figures would be high, but Nash was equally concerned about the "information assault" soon to be unleashed by "the opposing team" (propagandists) in Japan. The propaganda campaign of the Tokyo regime, Nash believed, had been more effective than Hitler's. The prewar "Asia for Asians" slogan and the war to liberate the Asian/ Pacific region from ruthless Western colonization had made an impact in the Far East at one time. Nash predicted that during the invasion Tokyo would play on America's tiredness of war and beg Asian Americans and other ethnic groups to reject Truman's so-called racist crusade against Japan. They would insist that unconditional surrender remained a bloody political mistake. Only headstrong presidential leadership and determination would offset this propaganda offensive, Nash said, and therefore all presidential waffling would have to stop immediately. In fact, he urged Truman to make public statements warning the American people about the self-serving nature of the nasty Tokyo propaganda to come. "Be on guard," should be the president's strong, consistent message, Nash insisted: "Japan is now fighting for a stalemate with the hope of negotiating a peace which will preserve the authority of its government and its ability to start another war under circumstances more favorable to Japan. Part of this fight for a negotiated peace is enemy propaganda encouraging movements for an early end of the war short of unconditional surrender. Informed Americans will recognize for what they are these efforts to cultivate support for a

the entire and final assault against Japan. The Army Department opposed this Congressional action, noting that millions of men now in Europe would soon be transferred to the Pacific. Placing an admiral in charge of what this huge army planned to do, they said, was illogical. But a new special rank for General MacArthur, of course, they deemed logical, leading a coalition of Congressional Democrats and Republicans to question their own fleet admiral decision.[28]

Secretary of War Stimson joined the debate, insisting that a new rank for the Army would be no easy accomplishment. John J. Pershing, the former commander of U.S. forces in Europe during World War I, was the only living American to hold a special military rank. His title was General of the Armies, and he was also the only American military figure in history to hold a rank beyond general. In 1799, the retired president and former Continental Army commander, George Washington, had been offered such a rank from Congress. He declined the honor.

Stimson's stress of technicalities implied to the press and others that the White House was making some sort of anti-MacArthur statement. The War Department's refusal to submit the names of any specific Army figures for the new rank added fuel to the fire. Truman commented that the country should be "more concerned about policy than personalities," but there would be many who believed then and for a long time afterward Governor Dewey's charge that both Roosevelt and Truman "never respected MacArthur."[29] This was a self-serving political statement, and it did nothing to rescue Dewey's 1944 and 1948 presidential bids.

At least on the surface, the combined chiefs of staff, who also met at the second Quebec (codenamed OCTAGON) conference, avoided debates over personalities and other political issues. Their major conclusion stressed the point that the Allies must "invade and seize objectives in the industrial heart of Japan." Yet U.S. Navy luminaries such as Admirals Ernest King and William Leahy were not convinced a full-blown invasion was necessary to accomplish this goal. "We could invade and seize," said King, once Japan, severely weakened by a grand, unprecedented naval blockade, was paralyzed by internal chaos, appeared on the edge of surrender, or simply surrendered.

King and Leahy (the chairman of the Joint Chiefs) had their disagreements on how Japan must throw in the towel, but neither of them considered a massive Allied invasion a necessary requirement for Japan's defeat. During an earlier, optimistic time, at the first Quebec conference (codenamed QUADRANT) in 1943, the combined chiefs of staff had agreed to defeat Japan within one year of the Nazi surrender. Nevertheless, defeating Japan and insisting on unconditional surrender were not the same thing to military strategists. Admiral King, for instance, believed that an invasion of southern Japan or Kyushu would only help the naval blockade and coinciding air assaults. Hence, his key to victory over Japan was blockade and bombing, and not a country-wide invasion.

While even Truman pondered the necessity of unconditional surrender now and then, the military's pondering involved the significance of the air war campaign over Japan, the impact of naval blockade, and differing Army vs. Navy strategies to humble the enemy. As late as the spring of 1945, neither the political community nor the military enjoyed a certain consensus over what must be done.

While the war dragged on, Admiral King took advantage of the time and planning period to launch attacks on small islands near the China coast and Formosa. This operation was initiated in the confidence that a full-scale invasion might not be necessary, for King continued to believe that General H.H. "Hap" Arnold's air war over Japan, plus the naval blockade, would win the war alone. Arnold, in the meantime, interpreted his post-OCTAGON orders to "intensify the air war" as Washington's way of saying that his bombers must humble Japan into a quick surrender. This could be done, he believed, and without hordes of invading ground troops. He continued to maintain this position long after the war was over. His little-read postwar tome, *Global Mission,* would be a passionate argu-

Atlantic Charter. The latter's commitment to democratic idealism was seen by many as America's best moment in World War II. But Stalin had little use for American idealism and Roosevelt had even less time to argue. Following the president's return to Washington from Yalta, the usually candid Roosevelt administration released only cryptic messages to the press in reference to Japan and Stalin. This would only add fuel to later controversies over Roosevelt's position at Yalta. Shortly after Truman took office, when decisions were being made on the Japan invasion, the American press was already asking questions about a rumored Kuriles Agreement with the Soviets. How could a nation dedicated to self-determination and decolonization offer an island chain to a tyrant? In a little-known or -remembered June 1945 news conference, and shortly before his own meeting with Stalin at Potsdam, President Truman dodged questions over Russian participation in a Japan invasion. He also denied that there were giveaways to the Soviets, and he urged the White House press corps to relax. The peace process after the war, he said, would remedy all controversies.[34]

The Yalta agreements were kept secret, Truman insisted, because the Soviets were not yet in the war against Japan. Any White House leaking of information which even implied a Soviet role in the Pacific war, he said, "might incite Japan to attack the Soviet Union." Such an attack would have especially injured the Soviets earlier in the year, Truman claimed, for they had focused their entire military effort on the final push to Berlin. This explanation was given in spite of Japan's known retreat and entrenchment, but the press had little interest in this particular aspect of the president's statement.[35] Truman's comments suggested what most everyone already suspected, i.e. that the Soviets would have some role in a coming Japan invasion. For the moment, the details were irrelevant. But the State Department thought the president had already been "too loose" with the press. In private communication with the White House, the State Department protested Truman's candor, noting that the Yalta conference was so hush-hush that the Secretary of State's office did not even have an official copy of the meeting's transcripts.[36]

Truman's commitment to candor was flexible. The press had no idea, for instance, that the president met with his top military aides on June 18, 1945, to "detail the campaign against Japan." This meeting of the minds had had two objectives. One was to make sure the president knew all the invasion details before talking to Stalin. Another was to make sure he understood that the military was not in unanimous agreement over the proper path to victory. The latter was something Truman did not want to hear. Dealing with a communist dictator was awkward enough, he said. Consequently, he had hoped his military people would present unanimous agreements to him. This would not be the case. In any event, he planned to ask the Soviets for "all the assistance in the war that was possible."

As always, so-called conclusive discussions on the Japan invasion raised more questions than conclusions. The impact of the Soviet role in that invasion became one of the larger questions at the June 18 meeting. According to the Yalta-set timetable, the Soviets would be entering the war against Japan in August 1945. For those supporting an air war/naval blockade approach alone, the Soviet entry represented another example of how a Japanese surrender could be won without a massive ground assault by Americans. But if the Japanese did not surrender because their old traditional enemy, the Russians, entered the war, and there were no U.S. troops on the ground in Japan to influence events, how could Washington ever dominate the postwar occupation government to come? Conventional wisdom suggested that Japan would not only surrender, but surrender quickly, upon the entry of the Russians. But if conventional wisdom was wrong and Japan fought on, the Red Army's advance, like in Eastern Europe, might soon represent a new era of Soviet imperialism. What a potential mess. Throughout the June 18 meeting, Truman heard more details and worst-case scenarios about this matter than anything else.

At the least the key spokespersons for various points of view on the invasion issue had gathered in one spot at one time for Truman's benefit. He was able to hear their best versions of what must or must not be done, and he insisted on tight, straight-

cans, the so-called Vichy regime was synonymous with puppet government and Nazi evil. Over 75 percent asked in a *New York Times* poll of 1941 demanded Leahy's recall and all U.S. connections to Vichy severed. Yet, Leahy believed that his own clever diplomacy could keep Vichy from moving even closer to Hitler and that, perhaps, he could someday win them to the Allied cause. At the least, he could try to convince Vichy-administered French North Africa to avoid shooting at the Allies once their invasion (Operation TORCH) began. He rarely met any success in his endeavors, but his commitment to diplomacy in the face of difficult challenges remained on track. Roosevelt, never a fan of Vichy's arrogant French alternative, Charles DeGaulle and his London-based Free French Resistance, had of course offered encouragement and support to Leahy throughout his mission. It all ended with TORCH in 1942. Three years later, Leahy believed Truman should take up the challenge of a settlement with the Japanese.[38]

Leahy "feared no menace from Japan in the foreseeable future," and therefore had little use for unconditional surrender. The latter was an unnecessary burden, he believed, and American forces would pay the price. Truman told Leahy that he had always tried to leave "the door open to Congress" if it wished to pursue some special settlement with the Japanese.[39] His comments implied that he would bow to their wishes if there was a significant, coordinated movement on Capitol Hill to abandon the unconditional surrender commitment. There was no such movement. There were also only a few rumblings in public opinion, and this was not the time, he said, to change peoples' minds.

The Kyushu invasion sounded "all right" to him, Truman told the June 18 meeting, and he authorized the Joint Chiefs of Staff to proceed. As soon as this invasion met success, then, he stressed, "a final action" would be determined. Truman said that he worried about "one Okinawa after another" during a Japan invasion. Hopefully, the enemy would surrender, but if they did not, then periodic June 18-like meetings would be required, the president suggested, to assess America's own resolve and its interests in peace versus military victory.[40]

In April 1946, several months after the Japanese surrender, those who would have led the invasion of Japan meet on the bridge of the USS *Franklin D. Roosevelt,* flagship of the Eighth Fleet. From left to right: Admiral Chester Nimitz, Admiral William Leahy, President Harry Truman, and Vice Admiral Marc Mitscher. (Courtesy of the Naval Historical Foundation and the National Archives)

During the critical time shortly before, during, and after the May 1945 surrender of Nazi Germany, a Normandy-like invasion of Japan was not a 100 percent given and the commitment to Japan's unconditional surrender was questioned. Yet, over fifty years later, the image of a forever focused, united, and resolute American government has become accepted fact. The media has especially helped in the creation of this legend. For instance, while offering a damning critique of President Bill Clinton's Kosovo policy, NBC reporter Brian Williams hosted an hour-long 1999 *Dateline* television news special analyzing America's "lost goals" in military and foreign policy. Williams,

continue the fight in Europe, the matter [naval transfer] would be given consideration." Hitler also insisted that he needed further consultations with Admiral Doenitz about the details of a potential transfer. If the "battle situation" improved, Hitler promised to send Japan "a submarine fleet" in the name of "cooperation." But there was no submarine fleet to dispatch.

With the Red Army in the streets of Berlin, the battle situation, of course, did not improve for Hitler. Furthermore, the Hitler-Doenitz consultations amounted to a minute or two of conversation. On April 20, 1945, Doenitz ordered "two or three submarines" to join up with the Japanese in the Pacific. He was not sure if any of the subs would accurately receive his orders, and he was less sure if there was enough fuel for these U-boats to make the long journey in the first place. One of those submarines, on the other hand, promised to get there, for it was already en route and carrying a pre-arranged German-Japanese technical assistance mission on board. The latter was the product of a "diplomatic offensive" led by Abe shortly before the final push of the Soviet military into Berlin.

The U-234, a large 1,600-ton submarine, had left Europe for Japan at the end of March 1945. It represented Hitler's best contribution to Japan during his final days. The technical assistance mission consisted of German experts in aerial defense and radar/radio-controlled weapons, two senior German naval officers to serve with the Japanese navy, two German civilian experts in the mass production of the experimental ME-262 turbo-jet fighter, and two Japanese naval officers who had been in Germany studying both jet fighter technology and high output submarine engines. Spotted by the U.S. Navy some five hundred miles east of Greenland, the U-234 surrendered without a fight. It was sailed to the large American navy base at Portsmouth, New Hampshire, but the two Japanese navy officers on board committed suicide before they could be interrogated.[2]

On April 20, 1945, Admiral Doenitz bid his final farewell to Adolf Hitler and headed to Flensburg near the Danish border. Abe went with him, informing Tokyo that the man soon to re-

place Hitler as the rightful ruler of Germany was a close personal friend whose judgment, leadership, and common sense
should be studied carefully. Apparently, Abe himself was not in
the mood for careful studying, for ten days after arriving in
Flensburg with Doenitz, he fled to Copenhagen just ahead of an
advancing British army. On May 5, 1945, with the Third Reich
entering its final hours, Abe and his staff won Doenitz's permis-
sion to head home to Tokyo. "With the greatest consideration,"
Doenitz said, an old German minesweeper was made available
to Abe and his staff of twelve in order to make a mad dash to
nearby Malmo in neutral Sweden.

From Malmo, Abe and the Japanese navy general staff in
Tokyo maintained a two-day correspondence about post-Ger-
man surrender resistance plans and the propaganda significance of what Tokyo assumed was Hitler's heroic death in Berlin.
Abe informed Tokyo that there were plenty of Nazis who planned
to fight on after the Allied victory. In time, they would restore
their beloved government, he predicted, and nothing would get
in their way. Consequently, Abe was ordered to study the planning behind the post-surrender Nazi resistance "in order to furnish reference material for the decisive battle awaiting Japan."[3]
Not yet knowing the details about Hitler's suicide, Abe's superiors assumed that the führer must have "died in battle defending his homeland." Abe was further ordered to find out the details,
for the tale of Hitler's heroic last stand would "inspire our countrymen to defend their own Capital when the time comes."

Whereas the details of Hitler's demise remained sketchy, the
Japanese government did hear a Honolulu-based radio broadcast that announced the German surrender proposal. The remaining Japanese naval commands in Batavia and Soerabaya
were ordered to take action against the German navy in South-
east Asia if it decided to surrender to the Allies. There were
believed to be six or seven German submarines in the entire Far
East, and the commander of one of them, speaking on behalf of
the German navy in the Pacific, informed the Japanese government that Doenitz's surrender had been deplorable. All Ger-

killed far away from Berlin, and during a coup led by Heinrich Himmler, the SS chief. Himmler had been involved in a last ditch peace feeler and, again according to the rumor, had asked Hitler to join the effort. When the führer refused, he was killed.

Foreign Minister Togo confirmed that Himmler had been involved in a peace mission behind Hitler's back. Hence the rumor of a coup was plausible. If true, it would be "inappropriate," he said, to announce it to the Japanese people. It would give them a certain precedent, Togo feared, to support a similarly-designed coup against their own government during the Allied invasion. Nothing, therefore, could be spoken about it. Hitler, the official announcement noted in Japan, had "fallen in Berlin."[6]

Were those in Hitler's government who had not "fallen" headed to Japan? This was an intriguing question, and Foreign Minister Togo wanted an answer. The Japanese minister in Berne, Switzerland, Shunichi Kase, was particularly concerned about the "Hitler exiles" issue, and Togo accepted his view. Kase pointed out that the press in Allied-liberated Europe was exposing Nazi atrocities on a daily basis. There was a "great deal of resentment," Kase said, toward the whole German people for the Nazi terror, and many believed that there was no difference between Germany and its ally, Japan. Vengeance was in the hearts of the Allies, Kase observed, and he predicted a very bloody Allied invasion whereby few Japanese civilians would be spared. Japan, he said, could prove to the Allies that it was different from Germany by refusing the entry of ex-Nazi leaders, or at least refusing them a government in exile while on Japanese soil.

Even if he was wrong about the vengeance matter, kindness to the Germans, Kase insisted, might result in even larger problems. The Soviet hatred of Nazis was legend. The last thing Tokyo needed to do, Kase stressed, was "invite" the Soviets to take part in the invasion of Japan. Togo agreed. The Soviet Union had no reason to remain neutral in the war against his country, unless, of course, domestic postwar reconstruction was to become the primary, singular goal of Joseph Stalin's regime. Togo hoped to convince Stalin of that necessity.[7] It would not be easy.

Worrying about the impact of the German surrender in Japan was one thing, but safeguarding the nation against a Soviet attack held the obvious priority. With the war in Europe now over, keeping the Soviets out of the war in the Pacific became the essential task of Japanese diplomacy.

As a priority matter, the Japanese Foreign Ministry informed its overseas diplomatic corps to make the following three issues clear to Soviet diplomats or to anyone who had the ear of Joseph Stalin. First, any German exiles arriving in Japan would be put under immediate surveillance and "all activities regulated by local authorities." Second, Japanese citizens would be forbidden from making any pro-Nazi or pro-"Hitler exiles" statements in public. And third, a Nazi government in exile would not be permitted in Japan or in Japanese-controlled territories.[8]

In reality, there would never be a Nazi exile problem for the Japanese government. But given the concern over a Soviet role in the upcoming invasion, it was important to make anti-Nazi statements as often as possible. Yet much of the discussion over German exiles continued to be based on wild rumor. One of the most intriguing tales involved a joint report from the Japanese military attaches in Germany that dated back to mid-April 1945. At that time, the attaches' dispatched a top secret memo to Tokyo about a German plan to fly a special JU-290 to Japan from Norway. The plane had nearly a six thousand-mile range at twenty thousand feet, and could make close to two hundred miles per hour. It would fly, according to this report, the so-called Great Polar Route to Japan with a four-man crew, senior Nazi government officials, and "one special passenger." The latter was believed to be Hitler himself who, the attaches' insisted, planned to set up a government in Japan whether his hosts liked it or not. Even specific dates for the flight were proposed, namely April 28, May 20, or June 15 (when the sun-moon angle would be at 90 degrees). This alleged escape plan could never be confirmed and was quickly rendered irrelevant, but the Japanese concern over the impending arrival of the once-vaunted Thousand-Year Reich lingered for weeks.[9]

cotts to invasion. Largely because of disagreements over the future of the Portuguese colony of Macau, Japanese-Portuguese relations were suffering anyway. Trying to live up to the prewar "Asia for Asians" and "Co-Prosperity Sphere" propaganda, Japanese officials in nearby Japanese-occupied Hong Kong constantly criticized the "Portuguese presence on Asian soil." In Macau, either anti-Japanese freedom fighters or organized crime operatives, depending on the story, had assassinated the Japanese Consul General there, Takashi Fukui, shortly before the Nazi surrender. While announcing the death of Hitler, Macau newspapers and radio newsmen even denounced Emperor Hirohito as a Hitler-like war monger. Japan was finished, they said. "Surrender now," the Macau press demanded, adding that Hirohito and "his clique" must be tried for war crimes. Both these demands and the assassination of the Japanese Consul General stimulated a wave of political violence in Macau throughout the spring and early summer of 1945. No one was safe, and the Soviet Union offered a way out.[12]

Although it must have been a strong ideological irony for Joseph Stalin's communist government, the anti-colonial Soviets assured the Portuguese colonial government that they would be there to "help" struggling, impoverished Macau after the war. The key, of course, was a Portuguese break in relations with the empire of Japan. Given the global nightmare of World War II, what Portugal did or did not do might have been considered irrelevant by the Japanese government. In reality, that government spent a considerable amount of time debating the significance of the Soviet involvement in the collapse of Portuguese relations. Foreign Minister Togo considered it just the beginning of an "evil pattern of events." How far should Japan go to keep Portugal as a so-called friendly listening post? The Japanese government was divided on the issue. Togo supported a list of apologies to the Portuguese in the interest of keeping some sort of foothold in Europe. The military opposed it, insisting that apologies to a "lesser Western colonial" was the height of dishonor.

Adding to Togo's Portugal position was his report that the Soviets were up to no good in other listening posts as well. Ireland was his loud and clear example. Little had disturbed Irish-Japanese relations over the years, and the assurances from the Irish government that it had no interest in entering the war against Japan had always been taken as "most sincere" in Tokyo. As Japan began its retreat to the home islands, there were several missionaries of Irish citizenry who were killed by Imperial Army troops. Not even this issue caused much a disturbance in what Foreign Minister Togo called "our gentle relationship."[13] The honeymoon ended in the spring of 1945.

Once again, the Soviet government was seen as the architect of the problem. The Irish government had made repeated assurances to Togo that it would never fight "side-by-side Stalinism." But the Japanese consulate learned that the Americans were lobbying hard for Irish entry, and that the Soviets were portraying themselves, at least in Ireland, as America's humble "junior partner" in the upcoming invasion of Japan. The Soviet government promised Ireland, Togo said, to act as a go-between during the invasion should there be any difficulty between Great Britain and Ireland during the invasion period. The Irish hatred for the British was as legendary as their friendliness toward the United States, and Togo predicted that Washington's and Moscow's parallel courtships of Ireland were destined to succeed. In his cabinet discussions, Togo complimented the Soviets and the Americans for their clever approach in dealing with the Irish, but he stressed the point that the Soviets were especially gifted in the matter. The Soviet Union had never been anyone's "junior partner," he pointed out, also predicting that Japan should expect more clever wheeling and dealing by the Soviets in the weeks to come. Not even the Vatican was safe from Moscow's influence, he believed.

If Catholic Ireland could be moved to join sides with the Soviet Union, then, Togo argued, the Vatican could not be too far behind. According to Kumao Harada, the Japanese consul general to the Vatican, a number of peace proposals had been

presented to Vatican officialdom. The authors of these proposals were shady, mysterious characters to Harada, including
multi-millionaires, Catholic humanitarians, and especially Soviet agents. In his correspondence with Togo, Harada could never
identify these individuals or their precise agendas. But he was
convinced that they did indeed exist and that they were all up to
no good. In any event, the details were irrelevant to Togo. His
larger mission was to inform the cabinet of Japan's growing
isolation and the significance of new Soviet- and Allied-led plots
against Japan. Anti-Japanese pressure on the Vatican, he said,
was another example.

Talking about peace, of course, was not unusual at the
Vatican, but the tenor and tone of the Vatican's communications with Harada had changed. Following the Nazi surrender,
the Papal Court insisted that Italian government internees in
the Far East must be released by the Japanese government.
The Court also charged that those Italian nationals had been
mistreated by their captors, warning that the Vatican was ready
to support the internment of Japanese citizens in Italy as a
matter of "just retaliation." This new demanding tone, both
Harada and Togo agreed, was the result of Japanese maltreat-
ment of Catholics in the Philippines throughout the Japanese
occupation there. The Vatican had issued a number of protests
to Tokyo over the matter, and Japan had either ignored or denied them. Now, Togo pointed out, the Vatican was getting its
revenge. The Japanese government, he said, should have been
more forthright with the Vatican, for it was in Tokyo's interest to
have the Pope on the side of "equitable peace for Japan." If the
Vatican was thinking about revenge, then, Togo reasoned, they
were ready to listen to a nation that had sought revenge against
Japan's Nazi ally and prevailed. That nation was the Soviet Union,
and the age-old conflict between Catholicism and communism
was suddenly irrelevant.[14]

Although based more on fear, rumor, and concern than hard-
core intelligence information, Togo's position moved the Japanese government to wage an aggressive last-ditch effort to head

off the collapse of Soviet-Japan relations. The newly intensified American bombing raids over Japanese cities added to the sense of doom, as well as aided his argument that something had to be done soon. Although Togo had welcomed most of his government's earlier wartime decisions, the foreign minister had been a loose cannon. He would pick and choose which offensive or military operation to endorse, and he once lost his job because of it. The need for diplomatic expertise brought him back to the cabinet, and, after the war, he would be able to claim, and with moderate success at his war crimes trial, that he had been a leading voice for peace throughout the history of the wartime government.

Persuading the Soviets to stay out of the Japan invasion was an impossible and ridiculous task, or so said the Japanese ambassador to the Soviet Union, Naotake Sato. The ambassador knew his host government well, and he claimed that Soviet-Japan relations had always fallen victim to Soviet duplicity, double-talk, and to the priorities of what Franklin Roosevelt had called the Allied Grand Coalition. In late May 1945, Togo's orders to Sato were urgent and clear. "Miss no opportunity to talk to Soviet leaders," Togo said, "as it is a matter of extreme urgency that Japan should not only prevent Russia from entering the war but should also induce her to adopt a favorable attitude toward Japan."[15] To Sato, these orders were "utterly meaningless," and there was "absolutely no hope" of stimulating Togo's requested "favorable attitude." Sato considered this response his "frank opinion," and apparently Togo distrusted him because of it. At least in the early summer of 1945 the Foreign Ministry in Tokyo did most of the contact work with the Soviets. It was not easy for Togo. In April 1945 the Soviets had abrogated their longstanding Neutrality Pact with Japan. To Sato it was only a matter of time until the Soviets announced "when their landing craft" would be approaching his country. Togo "counseled" Sato for his defeatist attitude, but the latter stayed on the job.[16] Meanwhile, the Foreign Ministry presented a three-point proposal to the Soviets.

6

Plan Versus Plan

By the late spring of 1945, nothing stood in the way of the Allied invasion of Japan. Most of the decisions had been made, and the facts and figures were set. The state of mind was another matter, and General MacArthur worried about how his troops felt about the battle to come. The fanaticism of the enemy was already well known, but the battle for Okinawa had especially illustrated how far the Japanese were willing to take the fight. Specifically, MacArthur worried about the significance and impact of the kamikaze. Did the upcoming American invasion face entire legions of kamikaze fanatics, or would the latter represent only a small percentage of the fight? Small percentage or not, MacArthur wanted to know what the kamikaze phenomenon was all about. The mass suicides on Saipan or banzai charges on Guam were one thing. Flying planes deliberately into both the Philippines and Okinawa invasion fleets was another, and MacArthur was concerned that his troops had seen nothing yet. In a fit of "know thine enemy" logic, the good general assigned a special Army intelligence task force to study the kamikaze, what made them tick, and what could the U.S. invasion really expect because of them.[1] This might have been deep background behind the specific invasion plans, but it was the most important deep background that MacArthur could think of on this eve of the attack. Sooner rather than later, the average GI would appreciate knowing some of these findings.

question. How had the Allies, if weak and corrupt, advanced to the gates of Japan? But centuries ago a "Divine Wind" or unexpected typhoon had saved Japan from a Chinese assault. In 1945, a human typhoon was expected to halt the American invasion. "The sooner the Americans come, the better. One hundred million die proudly." This was the new Tokyo radio–championed slogan of July 1945, and it was credited to the kamikaze of Okinawa. But the five survivors interrogated by Investigative Task Force #15 had never heard this slogan before. The patriotic legend of the kamikaze was growing by the day, and the Japanese government made certain of it.

MacArthur warmly acknowledged the hard work of Investigative Task Force #15, but it shed little light on his larger question. What was the level of fanaticism in Japan itself and what did it mean for the invasion?[4] Frankly, there would never be a satisfying or accurate answer. Without question, suicide attacks were part of the Japanese defense strategy.

With the bulk of Japanese forces killed, captured, or trapped overseas, and with the major cities facing daily bombing raids, an adequate defense plan was a grand challenge to the Japanese Imperial General Headquarters (IGHQ). On April 8, 1945, the IGHQ issued orders activating the First and Second General Armies of defense. An order activating an Air General Army was issued the following week. All home defense commands were centralized under one roof in the name of efficiency and coordination, and seven specific regional zones (nicknamed the "seven samurai") were created to carry on the fight. Code-named KETSU-GO ("Decisive Operation"), the first part of this defense plan involved destroying the American invasion before it hit the beach. Both night and day assaults on the invasion force were planned, and, if the landing force did hit the beach, it was of course to be destroyed there.

KETSU-GO was incredibly optimistic. While the lack of cooperation between the Japanese Imperial Navy and Army was legend throughout World War II, the government ordered all inter-service rivalry to cease throughout KETSU-GO. On the other hand, if the battle did indeed carry on into the interior, surviving defense units would join up with Civilian Defense Corps home guardsmen. Coordinating this link-up, even on paper, was a logistical nightmare for IGHQ. Had the American invasion taken place, KETSU-GO would still have been in the final planning stage.[5] The problems were obvious. First of all, each of the "seven samurai" regions had their own home defense plan. The Army and Navy might have been ordered to cooperate with each other, but provincial governors and city officials had no such orders. The latter often had their own ideas and plans for the grand defense, and it varied from town to town. Regional political leaders were reluctant to click their heels and obey a directive from a national government that had lost the war. They were suspicious of why the generals and admirals, most of them born and raised in northern Japan, were always so willing to sacrifice southern Japan.

Years after World War II, Fukushiro Nukaga, mayor of tiny Kajiki in Kyushu, remembered shouting at the top of his lungs at KETSU-GO planner Admiral Toyoda Soemu. Soemu expected the regional political community to follow his orders and selflessly support whatever he demanded of them and their electorate. But Nukaga had heard similar demands from another KETSU-GO planner, General Kawabe Mazakazu, who implied that Army requests came first in all matters of home defense. Caught in the middle, Nukaga balked at Admiral Soemu's suggestion that he would be shot for treason if he ignored Navy requests for civilian assistance in favor of the Army. Both the general and the admiral, Nukaga claimed, "talked down to him." In the view of these two northerners, Nukaga was a foolish country bumpkin anyway. But if civilian assistance was to play an equal share in the defense, Nukaga wanted to be considered as important to the cause as any admiral or general. The military, of course, disagreed.[6]

Many rumors abounded in Kyushu that certain government officials in Tokyo were already talking to the Allies about a peace deal. Would the destruction of towns like Kajiki be for nothing,

cave networks were required to house headquarters command, hospitals, and even reserve troops. And third, always maintain the high ground in order to avoid assaults by flame-throwing tanks.

Whereas the Americans always guessed that the adequate supplying of defense troops would be a Herculean effort for the Japanese, in reality the supply issue was not that critical to the KETSU-GO planners. KETSU-GO was not to be a long-term effort. The Japanese defenders had a three-month supply of ammunition, and that was it. Getting that ammunition to safe Kyushu caves and underground facilities was ordered during the early planning stages of KETSU-GO. So-called "high priority" areas, such as Kyushu, would receive the bulk of the three-month supply, while forces in other parts of the country would have to make do with meager amounts, as it was hoped that the Americans would bend and fold before the battle was carried beyond Kyushu. Amazingly, there was little discussion over what to do with the estimated 12,700 planes in Japan at the time. Few of them were military aircraft, and there were not enough pilots left alive to fly them. But most could be crashed into the enemy if enough kamikaze troops could be found to do it. As the invasion fleet arrived, KETSU-GO planned to unleash wave after wave of kamikaze planes. Three hundred planes constituted a wave. Nevertheless, at the time of the Japanese surrender, the level of pilot training had not reached this ambitious goal, and not all of those 12,700 planes were truly capable of flying.

The Japanese Navy's strongest contribution to KETSU-GO also came under the kamikaze heading. Only thirty-eight submarines were left in the home islands. Most of them would be outfitted with "kaitens," or suicide torpedoes. Their mission would involve the ramming and destruction of troop transport ships. They would be joined by five-man midget submarines, or "koryu." Although considered ineffective on the high seas, the midgets were now deemed invaluable by the Navy high command. They would only carry two torpedoes apiece, but that would be enough to cripple or sink a troop transport. Remaining Japanese indus-

tries were ordered to build koryu on a round-the-clock sched-
ule. The Navy wanted over five hundred midgets at the ready,
but this would prove to be an overly ambitious task. Getting so
many Navy personnel to commit suicide was not considered a
problem in KETSU-GO, although the plan admitted that finding competent sailors might be difficult. Similar kamikaze mis-
sions were assigned the remaining nineteen surface destroyers
and several patrol boats. Even the handful of Navy frogmen
were expected to train more frogmen in order to create an un-

In May 1945, a Japanese midget submarine of the type planned for
use in Operation KETSU-GO is placed on display at the Camp
Dealy rest camp on the island of Guam. The sub was later moved to
a bigger display area at Guam's naval station and is still there
today. (Courtesy of the Naval Historical Foundation and the National Archives)

on U.S. foreign policy to the Soviet dictator, Joseph Stalin. Whereas Roosevelt had favored a Grand Coalition with the Soviets in the name of postwar peace and detente, Truman was ill at ease with Roosevelt's Soviet policy. The U.S.–U.S.S.R. wartime alliance had been an expedient one. As early as 1939, the then Senator Harry Truman (D., MO) had denounced Stalin on the Senate floor as a "tinhorn dictator." Later, the folksy Truman once joked that the only difference between Hitler's Nazism and Stalin's Communism was that in Hitler's realm the innocent were killed in the name of the state. In Stalin's realm, they were killed for their own good.[12]

In time, the new president would develop his own confrontational style when dealing with the Soviets, but for the moment he was in a sense still learning the ropes. Potsdam was a difficult, challenging meeting for Truman, but he kept an immediate priority, the invasion of Japan, in clear focus. The Potsdam leadership promised the total destruction of Japan if it did not surrender unconditionally, and the Japanese government responded via government-controlled radio that there would be no surrender.

Although the November 1 invasion date for OLYMPIC remained firm, there was also to be something of a pre-invasion on October 27. The 40th Infantry Division was ordered to take the small islands just to the west of Kyushu, and the 158th Regimental Combat Team was assigned to take the largest of these islands alone. Their mission involved setting up the groundwork for the November 1 invasion, such as constructing a seaplane base, making radar installations operational, erecting medical facilities, and identifying and readying emergency anchorages for damaged invasion craft. Once this was accomplished, the U.S. Navy would arrive offshore Kyushu. Under Admiral "Bull" Halsey's personal command, the Third Fleet would include battleships capable of heavy bombardment and aircraft carriers capable of launching hundreds of planes. Halsey had promised to ready sixty-six carriers for the invasion. Meanwhile, Admiral Raymond Spruance's Fifth Fleet would sail the invasion force to their landing zones, and over three thousand ships were assigned to this task. They were supposed to arrive following a "ceaseless shoreline bombardment" by Halsey's destroyers and planes. The shelling, of course, would cease, but just moments before the first landing craft hit the beach.

The beaches of the primary landing zone on Kyushu's east coast near Miyazaki were codenamed after great American automobiles (BUICK, CADILLAC, CHEVROLET, CHRYSLER, CORD), plus one English car maker thrown in for Allied good measure (AUSTIN). It was here where the 25th, 33rd, and 41st Infantry Divisions were expected to advance, capturing Miyazaki city and Miyazaki airport. Another invasion group, consisting of the Americal Division, the 43rd Division, and the 1st Cavalry Division, would land just to the south of the Miyazaki area. Once again, the landing beaches were codenamed after existing and defunct American car companies, and this time without a token British manufacturer (DESOTO, DUSENBERG, ESSEX, FORD, FRANKLIN). Shibushi and Kanoya were the objectives here.

On the western shore of Kyushu, the Marine Corps' 2nd, 3rd, and 5th Divisions were assigned the capture of Sendai (not to be confused with the large, thriving port city of the same name in Japan's northern Tohoku province) and the historic port city of Kagoshima (where Japan had stood tall against foreign invasions in its ancient past). The Japanese defense was anticipated to be especially brutal here, given the area's combined economic, strategic, and historic significance. Despite its amazing heroism on Guam and elsewhere in the Pacific, the 3rd Marine Division was largely declared "expendable" in OLYMPIC. No or few survivors were expected. Famous for "taking the point" and prevailing in one island battle after another, the 3rd's hardened experience and expertise was needed again. Truman was shocked that the entire division might soon fight its last battle, but whatever they could do to beat back the bulk of a fanatical enemy was the bottom line for the Joint Chiefs of Staff.[13] After the war, Truman made a special visit to the 3rd Marine command headquarters, offering special praise for their suc-

supposed to take them into Yokohama, Tokyo's port city neighbor. Those landing just to the south of Tokyo included the 6th, 8th, 24th, 31st, 32nd, 37th, 38th, and 87th Infantry Divisions and the 13th and 20th Armored Divisions. All of this was considered the "initial assault."

The 2nd, 28th, 35th, 91st, 95th, 97th, and 104th Infantry Divisions (along with the 11th Airborne Division) were slated for a second landing after the initial assault. Few CORONET planners saw this as sufficient. More troops, CORONET concluded, were needed from training camps in the United States and from occupation duties in Europe. "Most likely," CORONET pointed out, these men would represent the final push into Tokyo, but this part of the plan was fuzzy on details. The exact number of final push troops and their specific redeployment orders from the United States and Europe had yet to be worked out. Meanwhile, victory in Tokyo did not necessarily mean the end of CORONET. The attack plan listed a number of "assumptions," and one of them was the Joint Chiefs of Staff conclusion that armed resistance in northern Japan was likely. From its new foothold in Tokyo, the Americans were expected to crush that resistance as well. Since this assumption ran headlong into the hope that Japan would surrender before the last American flag was raised over Tokyo, the Joint Chiefs avoided attaching any estimated date to the end of northern resistance in the original CORONET plan.[16] Obviously, CORONET was more the mixture of hope and assumption than OLYMPIC.

But most of CORONET's assumptions were logically based on battlefield experience and captured intelligence information. For instance, the Tokyo area population, CORONET predicted, would be more "fanatically hostile" than even the Civilian Volunteer Units faced in OLYMPIC. It was also assumed that the Tokyo defenders would do everything they could to bring up reinforcements. The endless American bombing raids would make that difficult, but not impossible. Both bombardments and the pressure from the initial landing forces were expected to keep the reinforcement rate to under four arriving divisions per week. These would have to come from within Honshu itself, for CORONET "guaranteed" {with one exception) that Japanese troops from the Asian mainland would never make it back home to Japan. The one exception involved a possible suicide attack staged by Japanese units in China. Finally, it was assumed that the fanatical Japanese defense would be most apparent in the early days of the American landings, but would wither as supplies, especially food, dwindled.[17] Time was on the American side, although a long battle might mean mass starvation in the civilian population. In short, the CORONET plan raised questions and concerns as it charted its attack priorities, never diminishing the significance of the horror and misery to come. Those concerns dated back to the early political wrangling during the days before precise invasion code names and landing sites were set. Setting landing zones was the easy part. Anticipating everything from guerilla resistance to civilian starvation was another matter.

Even more than OLYMPIC, the CORONET plan's underlying tone of dread and horror might have been one of the factor's influencing President Truman's decisions at Potsdam. U.S. military intelligence continued to augment original OLYMPIC and CORONET estimates of enemy strength, suggesting more and more the gruesome fight to the death. Continually adjusted Tokyo defense preparation reports became especially nightmarish. Because of this fact, the direct correlation between all this frightening, last-minute data and President Truman's decision to drop the atomic bomb has always fascinated anyone interested in the end of World War II. The answer, on the other hand, has never been satisfying to the serious student of the matter, for a precise blow-by-blow record of the president's decision-making does not exist. For instance, eight years after World War II, James Cate, an Air Force historian, wrote ex-President Truman asking him what truly happened. Truman replied that he remembered talking to General Marshall shortly after learning about the successful testing of America's nuclear weapon. Together, he said, they weighed the significance and meaning of

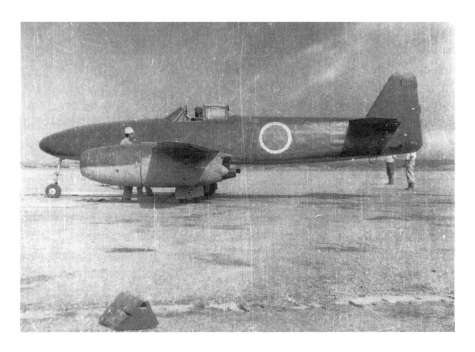

The Nakajima Kikka ("Orange Blossom"), Japan's first jet-powered aircraft. (Courtesy of the National Air and Space Museum)

Its second test resulted in a flaming disaster. There was no third attempt.

Even greater hope had been placed in the Kyushu J7W Shinden. This new plane left its production factory less than two weeks before the end of the war. Expected to be ready weeks before the feared American invasion, the Shinden ("Magnificent Lightening") represented a possible mass production aircraft in contrast to the other high-tech wonders. Deemed a "pusher-propeller aircraft," the Shinden was a rear-engined plane. Its engine produced over 2,100 hp, driving a stern propeller close behind the cockpit. An odd-looking lightweight machine, the Shinden was designed to be an interceptor fighter plane with a top speed in the 460 mph range. That meant it was slightly faster than America's P-51d fighter plane. It was the only aircraft of its type built by any nation during World War II, and it was expected to carry four 30mm cannon in its nose.

According to postwar statements by their designers, both Shusui ("Sword Stroke") and Kikka ("Orange Blossom") had been modeled off of Germany's early World War II Messerschmitt fighter planes; however, during the war, these planes were described as unique and "inspired" Japanese-only inventions. The Shinden, on the other hand, had been truly a Japanese-only design. It just came too late to meet its wild mass production timetable.

Only one of the four grand inventions would ever see combat, and it would indeed be in the kamikaze category. The Yokosuka MXY7 Ohka, or "Cherry Blossom," was dubbed a "piloted missile." Deliberately designed as a high-tech kamikaze weapon, the Ohka carried a 2,600-pound warhead in the tip of its nose. Resembling a miniature glider, the plane was distinguished by its twin-tipped airfoil or rear wing, unusually short wingspan, and cherry blossom monograms instead of the usual Rising Sun. Dropped from a bomber, the tiny Ohka could race to its target at 600 mph. It was the first of the big four techno weapons to be constructed, and nearly 800 of them were built by the end of the war. In fact, the first Ohka attack took place during the early days of the Okinawa invasion in April 1945, and an American destroyer was hit straight on. KETSU-GO called for even faster, more heavily armed Ohka to be readied for the American invasion of Japan. But these "ultra" versions of the original "piloted missile" remained only on paper, on plans discovered by accident in a Kyushu cave several years after the war.[20]

To longtime MacArthur friend and OLYMPIC/CORONET senior planner Brigadier General Frederick P. Munson, the American military and government never respected or appreciated Japan's technological potential. In April 1945, Munson had been especially concerned about the appearance of the Ohka and made the most noise about it in official circles. He also worried about what Japan might have invented in the area of tanks and shore batteries, and he could not get a straight an-

by old men and children. Moreover, how would U.S. troops re-act to their own introductions of horror? Stillwell had been an early advocate of chemical warfare in OLYMPIC, and 1945 chem warfare experiments in the United States had proven more ef-fective in rooting out or killing cave-based defenders than any other weapon. During the invasion, gas was expected to make its first real appearance as an available offensive weapon in World War II. Matters of ethics and even international law violations had troubled Munson more than Stillwell about the use of gas, but he learned that the postwar Stillwell was very relieved that America never had to lead the way in modern gas warfare. Its use would have hurt America's later role as the moral and ethical democratic leader during the Cold War, he said. After the war, Stillwell even doubted that his U.S. army troops would have been adequately outfitted to protect themselves from their own gas attacks. Invasion planning always moved faster than these needed supplies, although General Marshall had promised an efficient supply line in all situations. Munson and Stillwell found it inter-esting that Marshall never offered guarantees, just promises.[24]

Since OLYMPIC/CORONET never took place, it has been an easier task than normal for former participants to reinterpret their roles over the years. Mike Mansfield once predicted that the tale of the Japan invasion would always remain mysterious because of it. This feisty, former Montana Senator, Senate ma-jority leader, and ambassador to Japan for Presidents Jimmy Carter and Ronald Reagan had been attached to the U.S. House of Representatives Subcommittee on Naval Affairs shortly after World War II. He first reviewed the still-classified OLYMPIC/CORONET plans at that time, and for the record wrote the first Congressional acknowledgment of the existence of these plans. Quickly becoming one of the country's top experts on Japanese policy, Mansfield, some Capitol Hill wags used to joke, spent more time in Tokyo than Helena. Nevertheless, Mansfield was struck early on by what ex-invasion planners said they did, or meant to do, versus what the record suggested.[25]

To Mansfield, the invasion plans had the makings of a disaster for the United States. Ranging from potentially high desertion rates and even mutinies to lack of command coordination and cooperation, Mansfield read a lot of gloom and doom between the lines of OLYMPIC/CORONET. This was, Mansfield admitted, "yet another God-damned interpretation," and that was the point. These plans were the products of endless argument and debate, and long after they were penned controversy would still reign.

In the big picture, Mansfield saw a high degree of arrogance in the invasion plans. His old friend Harry Truman, he believed, had expected too much of America's youth to die by the tens of thousands in faraway Japan. More thought should have been given to modifying the unconditional surrender demand, he insisted. Meanwhile, the issue of race troubled him too. In Europe, the war had always been against Hitler and the evil Nazis. In the Pacific, the war was against the nation of Japan and an enemy race. Were the invasion plans, he asked years later in the 1970s, an effort to defeat the Japanese military or to "eradicate the Japanese race"? He doubted that the surviving ex-planners could ever offer a straight answer. Although many of his comments during his heyday as an American foreign policy maker were influenced by the then ongoing Vietnam War (which he opposed), Mansfield had made identical observations thirty years before.[26] If anyone was consistent in his views and concerns, it was Mansfield, and he won accolades from the Japanese while serving as U.S. ambassador because of this honest, no-nonsense approach.[27] Mansfield's long-held view that the war against Japan had been a race war was strongly echoed in the 1980s and 1990s by Pulitzer Prize–winning historian John Dower in books with titles like *War Without Mercy* (1986) or *Japan in War and Peace* (1993).

Although everyone and their uncle involved in the invasion planning process seems to have had a strong opinion on what really happened, the following matters, at the least, cannot be debated. The invasion plans were never implemented, the A-bombs were dropped, and Japan surrendered.

7

The A-Bomb Debate

In Italy during late July 1945, *The Stars and Stripes* reported that a new song was sweeping through the ranks. It would never make the Hit Parade, but its lyrics expressed a certain sentiment and exhaustion that, according to the press, should worry invasion planners. Nicknamed "The Truman Song," its composer was believed to be a former music student from New York, Pfc. LeRoy W. Goyer: "Please, Mr. Truman, won't you send us home? We have captured Napoli and liberated Rome; We have licked the master race, And now there's lots of shipping space. So won't you please send us home? Let the boys at home see Rome."[1]

Nevertheless, that same issue of *The Stars and Stripes* told its military audience how American troops heading home would also head to Japan. Stopping off in the States before the Japan invasion was not to be expected. Those European veterans lucky enough not to be shipped immediately to the Pacific would have little time to enjoy their Stateside furlough. Twenty-two "personnel reception stations" were to be scattered across the United States, and all of them were important railheads. The European theater veterans would be shipped to the reception station closest to their homes, and if their loved ones were still too far away to reach, family members were expected to come to them. This was easier said than done, but the Pullman train company especially promised efficient round-the-clock service. They also guaranteed the Truman administration that all furloughed troops could be shipped to West Coast embarkation points in six days if necessary. The White House found the promise inadequate, but also wanted an undetermined number of in-transit veterans to enjoy a furlough "for reasons of psychological necessity."[2] Whether furloughs should be granted at all, and particularly in light of the specific invasion plans, was under debate in the Pentagon when the A-bomb decision was made.[3]

To Pfc. Goyer, the most important matter in his life during

In August 1945, the ships of the U.S. Third Fleet steam toward Tokyo Bay. (Courtesy of the National Archives Still Pictures Branch)

July 1945 was being able to see his fiancé again before moving on to the Japan invasion. He had no problem telling the press that he was not alone in the hope that "decent R & R" would be granted to European theater veterans like himself. It was the right thing for the new president to approve, he believed, and he joked that even Japanese troopers "must be wanting some time about now" as well.[4]

Goyer was right. There were plenty of Japanese who believed that it was time for a rest. One of them was a wounded ex-Imperial Army soldier, Sumiteru Taniguchi. Eking out an existence as a part-time postal delivery man in the summer of 1945, Taniguchi believed that teenage veterans like himself had already given their all to the nation. It was time to step back, relax, and consider the options to a futile defense. He kept his opinions to himself, but that would change after the war. Born and raised in Nagasaki, Taniguchi would be a lucky survivor of the August 9, 1945 atomic bomb blast. Coming three days after the destruction of Hiroshima, the weapon in this second attack was nicknamed "Fat Man." It blew Taniguchi off his bicycle, and the force sent him flying over a fence into a garden. When he got up some time later, he had lost his hearing and his neighborhood. Only dust and rubble remained of his old mail route. His hearing would return by the end of the day: "I remember a flash of light and a big bang. The ground was shaking for a long time. Later I walked 200 yards uphill. Then I collapsed. I was so weak, but I felt no pain. I saw many bodies, but couldn't tell if they were men or women. People were dying in the street. It was all so unreal. At that time my skin had still not come off."[5]

Fifty-five years later, Taniguchi argued that his government should have surrendered earlier in 1945 instead of moving forward with KETSU-GO. In 2000, and already in his mid-seventies, Taniguchi founded a compensation movement for Nagasaki survivors, expanded it to include Hiroshima victims the following year, and made headlines in Japan for not demanding money from the Americans. Instead, he blamed Japanese authorities for his misery, urging the government of then-Prime Minister

Yoshiro Mori to pay for all medical expenses of all Nagasaki/ Hiroshima survivors. Arguing that the wartime government had by its own horrific actions pressured the Americans to use the atomic bomb, the present Japanese government's nonresponse to the still suffering people of Hiroshima and Nagasaki, Taniguchi said, was shameful and unforgivable. The Americans, he also argued, had no alternative to the bomb. "No caring American leader," he insisted, would have ever unleashed an invasion against "crazy men" in Japan when a "super weapon" was available to end the war.[6]

This call for compensation as a matter of wartime atonement won the endorsement of the major Tokyo newspapers. But Taniguchi's appeal came at a time of economic recession, political scandal, and hot debate over Japan's role in World War II. The "Taniguchi Issue," as it came to be known, offered a different spin to the usual argument over the morality and ethics of America's use of the A-bomb.[7] Taniguchi's contention that Truman was justified in dropping the bomb was politically incorrect to many of his generation, and the latter still held the reigns of political and business power in Japan. At the Peace Memorial in Hiroshima and in classrooms across Japan, the Truman administration had been denounced for using the bomb. Taniguchi, one man with one cause, helped refocus the matter.

According to 2001 Japanese government figures, there were 297,000 survivors in the vicinity of the Hiroshima and Nagasaki blasts. Trying to certify payment for medical costs incurred since 1945 has equaled a bureaucratic nightmare for all of them. Taniguchi was one of those given the bureaucratic runaround, even though doctors told him that he was lucky to be alive. He had been only one mile from ground zero when "Fat Man" exploded fifteen hundred feet above the Catholic cathedral at Urakami, just outside of Nagasaki. In fact, this had not been the U.S. aircrew's primary target. It was supposed to be Kokura, an industrial suburb of Nagasaki, but thick cloud cover also clouded the attacking B-29's visibility. Hence, it flew on to the secondary target, the Mitsubishi shipyards in Nagasaki. At first the visibility issue remained a problem. Clouds also covered Nagasaki, but a small break in the clouds allowed the B-29 to spot the Mitsubishi Armaments Works at Urakami. "Fat Man" was released.

The blast utterly destroyed Urakami and most of Nagasaki. The resulting fireball melted glass and even bricks, the effects of which can still be seen today. Although historians and Japanese government officials argue over exact casualty figures or when someone died "instantly," it is generally accepted that some 40,000 people died in Nagasaki on the day of the blast. But the rest suffered a long, painful death due to the varying effects of radiation poisoning. Anyone within 1.3 miles of ground zero suffered severe burns. Taniguchi was one of them, but it took weeks for much of his skin to peel off. He never received medical treatment at the time, for there was no medical personnel in his area. Taniguchi's grandfather dabbed cooking oil on the burns, and he lived off boiled persimmon leaves and vinegar for days. Since the food supply was believed to be permanently poisoned, this home remedy approach to radiation recovery seemed to make sense at the time.[8]

Most of his burns were on his back, and Taniguchi eventually spent twenty-one months laying on his stomach in a makeshift hospital. He learned of his government's surrender days after it took place, and he spent an additional thirty months in and out of special radiation treatment centers. But Taniguchi would go on to live a normal life, joking years later that his chain-smoking habit would kill him before the leftover effects of "Fat Man." He returned to his mail carrier work and spent the next fifty years on the job. His family spent several years trying to arrange a marriage for him, and a match was eventually found. Although his wife feared their two children would suffer horrible genetic defects, there have been no health problems at all for them. Taniguchi became a grandfather and built his Nagasaki/Hiroshima survivors organization only weeks after his long overdue retirement. Even though he was suddenly a nationally recognized figure, Taniguchi could not afford his medical expenses. He was under no illusions that his organization would succeed in anything but making headlines: "Some Japanese people argue we should pressure the United States for money. Personally, I feel even if we receive more money those who lost their lives will not return. But rather it is our duty to let people know what happens when you use nuclear weapons."[9]

In the "it's us or them" mentality that governed White House A-bomb decision-making, it is unlikely that President Truman spent much time wondering about the possible effects of the bomb on men like Taniguchi. Ever since Truman's days of decision, an entire field of study has been created over the significance of what Truman did or did not do. Professional historians, such as Gar Alperovitz, Samuel J. Walker, and Stanley Weintraub, have offered especially intriguing books within the recent 1990s literature alone.[10] Given the nuclear horror of Hiroshima and Nagasaki, opinions will always vary over Truman's precise motives and intentions. Meanwhile, even the latest declassified information tells a familiar tale that has been told, revised, and told again.

The U.S. atomic bomb project began exactly six years before the projected invasion date of Japan. Dr. Albert Einstein, the famous physicist, and several of his colleagues informed the White House about the potential military use of nuclear science. In correspondence with the president, Einstein warned of Nazi Germany's interest in that same military use, and that the United States must not waste any time of its own. But America's atomic bomb project started small in October 1939, only later expanding into the expensive $2 billion Manhattan Project. Including many German Jewish refugees, like Einstein, who had fled Nazi Germany, the Manhattan Project combined the talents of both civilian and military researchers. How to use the product of their efforts was a different story, and the decision process began in the spring of 1945.

When Harry Truman entered the Oval Office, the war in Europe was almost over. Although a good New Dealer, he had never been in Roosevelt's inner circle. He was not even informed about the Manhattan Project until the twelfth day of his presidency. In an almost cryptic fashion, Secretary of War Stimson told him about a top secret matter that was destined to have a dramatic impact on U.S. defense and foreign policies. Stimson also recommended a Hot Springs/Presidio-like committee of scientific, military, and political experts to decide how or if the bomb should be used. Truman agreed, and the committee soon recommended an attack on Japan without warning. Reminiscent of the Hot Springs–styled divisions and arguments, a coalition of young scientists disagreed with this recommendation. They suggested that Truman put on a nuclear demonstration, testing the bomb on a deserted island in full view of America's allies. Then a surrender demand would be made on the Japanese, warning them of horrible destruction if they did not comply. If the Japanese still refused a peace, and if Allied governments and public opinion were united in the decision to use the bomb, the military would be ordered to do the job.

Secretary Stimson countered this conclusion by setting up another committee. The latter rejected a special test of the bomb and had little confidence that harsh warnings to Japan would make any difference. Particularly if the desert island test failed, the resulting U.S. embarrassment, they predicted, would have an unfortunate impact on U.S. policy for years to come. By June 1945 the loudest message that Truman heard came from this corner. But was the bomb necessary for the Japanese surrender? The debate rages on, and the "yes" and "no" answers continue to haunt a curious world.

Although there are many versions of the "yes" versus "no" debate, two responses, at least, have emerged as the most acceptable in recent years. Naturally, one school of thought gives Harry Truman the benefit of the doubt. It supports the president's view that the atomic bomb saved America from the horrible invasion, led to the Japanese surrender roughly one week after the first bomb was dropped, and gave Emperor Hirohito the political edge to persuade the sword rattlers in the Japanese government to accept their fate, keep the nation alive, and think

would have been an early surrender that made the A-bomb unnecessary. Even Britain's legendary Winston Churchill, who was defeated for reelection during the middle of the Potsdam conference, became a quiet critic of unconditional surrender. Too many lives were lost, he complained, because of it. Later, he also noted that the A-bomb decision was made by too many newcomers to vital wartime policy-making. For instance, the new U.S. Secretary of State, James Brynes, was less knowledgeable about Asian/Pacific matters than Roosevelt's long-reigning chief of the State Department, Cordell Hull. And along with Truman and Britain's new prime minister, Clement Attlee, the new team did not have much time to be freshmen.[12]

On July 16, 1945, Truman learned that the first test of the atomic bomb had been successful. The Joint Chiefs, supported by Stimson, advised the president to postpone any offer to Hirohito until the atomic bomb had been dropped on Japan. The first target, Hiroshima, had been spared from previous bombing raids, preserving it as a test site for the atomic bomb. A city of over 250,000 people and few military targets, some 80 percent of its buildings were destroyed by the bomb. General MacArthur's headquarters estimated the death toll at 78,000, labeling it "enormous"; however, the Japanese Welfare Ministry estimate was closer to the mark. They said over 66,000 died immediately or within three months after the blast, and another 69,000 in the area were injured, missing, or dying of radiation sickness. Twenty-three American POWs were among the dead.

Truman was pleased that yesterday's experimental weapon might win World War II today. The world had just witnessed the "greatest thing in history," he claimed, and he couldn't be "happier about any announcement he had ever made." One week before they had originally planned to do so, the Soviets announced their entry in the war on August 8, 1945. Taniguchi-san and his neighbors would suffer the Nagasaki blast twenty-four hours later. The once jubilant Truman was somber. Explaining to his cabinet that "wiping out" more thousands in a third atomic attack was now "too horrible" to contemplate, the president canceled plans to do so. Conventional bombing attacks were stepped-up, making the last day of fighting in World War II one of the most intense bombing campaigns of the Pacific war. Breaking with tradition, and daring to set a new precedent of direct cabinet involvement, Emperor Hirohito on August 10 ended the government's deadlock on the issues of surrender and peace. Japan now accepted the Potsdam Declaration on the sole condition that the emperor be retained. Truman agreed, also reversing America's position of "no deals." Hirohito went to work again, urging his Imperial Conference (and the nation) to "bear the unbearable" and accept defeat. He, his closest associates, and much of Japan wept after this public statement was made. An estimated one thousand military officers, unable to live in a world of dishonor, committed suicide in the Tokyo area alone. The war ended on August 14 and the surrender ceremony took place on September 2.[13] But the debate had just begun.

Truman and Stimson claimed that no A-bomb use meant unacceptable casualties in the planned invasion. But the wisdom of this conclusion was even questioned at the time. At Potsdam, the Allied commander in Europe, General Dwight Eisenhower, argued that the Japanese were moments away from surrender and that A-bombs were not needed to "save American lives." This U.S. Army view from Europe was bolstered by the U.S. Navy view from the Pacific. In many respects, the Navy had not changed its position from the early invasion-planning days. In fact, the Navy's position paper offered at Potsdam stressed the point of Japanese desperation. With Japan blockaded from all overseas contact, and American battleships shelling Japan at will, the Suzuki government had no other option but to surrender, the Navy explained. Even MacArthur admitted that Japan was truly on the ropes, and the crusty self-proclaimed air power expert, General Curtis Lemay, said that Japan was "dead and gone" long before the atomic bomb attacks. The Pentagon's immediate postwar study of the A-bomb decision, part of the U.S. Strategic Bombing Survey, echoed all these concerns. The Survey concluded that the Japanese would have

Americans that global nuclear destruction was a very real possibility in their lifetime, and that maybe a Cold War could never be won on a battlefield. A nuclear test ban treaty was signed, but the nukes never went away. The effort to symbolize America's continuing anti-communist commitment (minus the stress on nuclear diplomacy) ended up being the long, tragic war in Vietnam. The latter also put the A-bomb debate on hold while the country divided up over what role its conventional forces should play, if any, in the Third World.

The collapse of the Soviet Union and communist China's rush to adopt capitalist-like reforms also brushed aside significant public concern over the possibility of a nuclear holocaust. But that concern always lingered beneath the surface. By the mid-1990s there was a certain mood of reflection over America's nuclear past. Because of it, there was also a general consensus in the historical profession and in the interested press that the time had come to focus the A-bomb debate and make some sense of its many arguments.

The mid-1990s marked the fiftieth anniversary of the use of the bomb. Japan had begun a wrenching and overdue debate in reference to its role in World War II, and neighboring Asian/Pacific countries watched it closely. From the pages of Tokyo's most important daily newspaper, *Asahi Shimbun,* to controversial films (such as 1998's blockbuster *Pride: The Fateful Moment* about the postwar war crimes trial of Prime Minister Hideki Tojo) to special Hiroshima/Nagasaki conferences at Waseda University and Tokyo University, many Japanese sought the truth and not propaganda. Back in Washington, both the White House and Congress struggled to find a new post–Cold War foreign policy, and public opinion was more curious than ever about how the Cold War had truly started. According to the polls, most of the voters supported fewer nuclear weapons. On the new computer-based Internet, websites about the atomic attacks on Hiroshima and Nagasaki grew on both sides of the Pacific, widening the discussion like never before. Meanwhile, aging and dying World War II veterans, now lionized by their children and grandchildren as "the greatest generation," sought answers and maybe some peace over what happened in Japan on August 6 and 9, 1945. Finally there was some focus and discipline to the A-bomb debate. It was better late than never.

Did hundreds of thousands of people in Hiroshima and Nagasaki have to die in August 1945? Adding depth and insight to this answer had always been a challenge for the analysts, because it remained one of the few historical questions whereby a very precise response was of paramount importance. That meant going over and over again what was generally known to be true, and then finding the rest of the story. In addition to the archival documents on the A-bomb decision, nearly all of the senior policy-makers of the time published postwar memoirs of their involvement in this matter. Contradictions existed in that literature, but many of those problems have been cleared away. That did not mean the debate was over, and lingering questions still characterize the A-bomb decision analysis.

Over the years there has been a considerable degree of discussion over what President Truman did or did not do on the night of July 21, 1945. Truman had learned of the atomic bomb test five days earlier, but he received a detailed report from General Leslie Groves on the twenty-first. The report's arrival coincided with the president's review of military intelligence reports that indicated more Japanese troops in defensive positions throughout Kyushu than previously believed. This revelation seems to have been a last straw for Truman, who then ordered General Carl Spaatz to Guam to take command of the Strategic Air Forces in the Pacific. The orders also instructed him to "deliver a Special Bomb" after August 3. That order was supposed to have been further approved by General Marshall and Secretary Stimson. There has been debate over whether Truman had truly won their approval at that time, and the very asking of this question suggests a certain singular and hurried determination on Truman's part to drop the bomb. There is no evidence to support claims of such overly anxious behavior.[17]

On the other hand, if the Kyushu intelligence report was a

American and Soviet Chiefs of Staff meet at Cecilienhof Palace during the Potsdam Conference. (Courtesy of the Harry Truman Library and Stock Montage)

he had strong views on all these matters before he arrived at Potsdam, and later information about the successful A-bomb test and Japan's new Kyushu defense plans confirmed and amplified his approach.

One of the reasons for the element of mystery that still surrounds Truman's opinion, motivation, and objective during the A-bomb decision-making process involves his own behavior. Following Truman's A-bomb announcement to the press, the journalism profession had as many questions about A-bomb matters as later historians. Their queries were met with elusive, cryptic comments from the president and his staff. Granted, the war still raged on when the original questions were asked.

Security remained important. On the other hand, Truman did not answer the many technical questions, and he made light of his lack of scientific knowledge. For example, he joked that he had a hard time figuring out how to drive the late Franklin Roosevelt's handicapped-equipped Ford, much less dissecting the workings of an atomic bomb.[22] Such comments convinced later historians that Truman was too cavalier about the significance of the A-bomb. In any event, his folksy comments to the press were a Truman characteristic, and the smiles and laughter were due to the fact that a long, hideous war was finally coming to an end. Few berated him for it. The criticisms of the "callous Truman" would come years later.[23]

Truman had been on the job four months when the war ended. The press of the day found his "quiet candor and easy optimism" quite amazing under the circumstances. This onetime Missouri haberdasher had become the principal actor in one of history's greatest events. He broke the A-bomb and Soviet entry news to the press with gentle humor on board the cruiser *Augusta* during the voyage home from Potsdam. The president had just finished the last bite of a sandwich in the crew messroom when he stood-up, explaining that he had an announcement to make. Both U.S. military personnel and reporters stood when he did, everyone laughed, and he told them to sit down. Truman looked at the enlisted men when he said a bomb had been dropped on Japan "more powerful than 20,000 tons of TNT." They responded with cheers and yelling. The president was then invited to attend an outdoor smoker and an afternoon of crew-arranged entertainment. Truman spent the smoker in good humor, noting that he hadn't laughed so hard in years.[24]

When *Augusta* arrived in Newport News, Virginia, Truman had been away from home for over a month. Looking tanned and fit, the president left the ship to find John Synder, his administration's chief war mobilizer, waiting for him. The transition from a wartime to peacetime economy was now America's top priority issue, Synder said, and Truman agreed with him. Postwar economic planning was the topic of discussion through-

When General Seiichi Tanaka, Commander of the Eastern Army, learned of the plot, he raced with loyal troops to the Imperial Palace offices and secured the area. Earlier in the day the rebels had tried to enlist Tanaka's own staff. The staff's appearance beside Tanaka was enough to convince the conspirators to surrender. One of these rebels, Major Hidemasa Koga, was former Prime Minister Tojo's son-in-law. He committed suicide, as did two of the other plotters.

Hirohito had just gone to bed when the action began. Awakened and guarded for his own protection, the emperor paced his bedroom talking to himself. The latter was not unusual behavior for him during times of crisis. He asked his closest aide, Hisanori Fujita, "What on earth do these men have in mind? Why do they not understand how much this pains me?"[29] General Tanaka soon arrived to announce the quick end of the palace insurrection, and Hirohito praised him to the heavens for his success. But Tanaka still felt guilty for the very existence of the plot, took full responsibility for it, and committed suicide shortly afterward. Korechika Anami, the war minister, also committed suicide, hoping that his death would "atone for his crime." Anami, a tough veteran of the New Guinea campaign, had favored one last great battle against the Americans. Because of this position, anti-surrender rebels thought he might be one of them. Anami refused to participate in any rebellion, but he was torn by his loyalty to both the warrior's code and the emperor. Death was the only honorable way out of that personal hell.

There were sporadic acts of anti-surrender violence across Tokyo and Yokohama in mid-August 1945, and to this date the precise number and significance of these acts remains a matter of speculation and opinion. Some, like the Palace Revolt, are decently documented, although Japanese historians, such as Imperial Family expert Toshiaki Kawahara, claim that Western historians have exaggerated the tale for whatever reason. Although Kawahara's work is generally known by only a handful of Japan experts in the West, this economist-turned-historian has dedicated much of his career to studying the wartime to peacetime transition. To Kawahara, few "thinking Japanese" would have welcomed or tolerated a coup and the resulting anti-surrender government.[30] His is not, of course, the final word on the subject, and the debate goes on.

As far as America was concerned in mid-August 1945, Japan was finished. But what did that mean? Although the Truman administration's public comments allegedly favored a good round of national celebrating, they did not live up to their talk of joy and jubilation. The rest of the country seemed to have the same mixed bag reaction. In contrast to the wild national party over V-E Day in May 1945, the V-J Day celebrations depended upon the community. Most of the polls indicated that Americans were relieved versus overjoyed that the war against Japan was over. Although the issue was never squarely addressed in the polls, much of that relief had to do with the fact that the invasion of Japan never had to take place. Others told reporters that they worried about Japan's reaction to arriving U.S. occupation forces, and even others said "our boys" in the Pacific should still expect "a few kamikaze attacks."[31]

The truly wild celebrating of the peace was overseas. On Okinawa the news came at night. The entire sky near the island was filled with red tracers. Star shells followed moments later, then came the boom of the big guns. This amazing "fireworks" display went on for thirty minutes straight. Booze, if someone could find it, was passed along from one gunner to another. But the celebrating took its toll. When the shellfire was over, six American seamen were dead and fifty seriously wounded. In Manila, for two hours the city went delirious. For U.S. forces who had been there for awhile, and for those who had just arrived from Europe earmarked for the defunct invasion of Japan, the news of peace was greeted by partying in the downtown streets, machine-gun fire in the air, and the deafening roar of hundreds of car horns. Despite the look of spontaneity, this event had been planned for days. Or so General MacArthur said. At the end of two hours, military policemen moved into the city center, cleared the streets, and traffic returned to normal.[32] The party was over.

while, Japanese rightists have claimed that their willingness to resist an invasion has been too easily discounted by historians thanks to the peaceful cooperation between most Japanese and the American authorities during the occupation government period. The implication of these claims is that a successful guerilla movement awaited the Americans, but history suggests otherwise. Consequently, the "might have been" story continues to expand, often has a life of its own, and sometimes remains totally divorced from reality. The simple facts remain that an invasion appeared necessary at a critical time, almost was launched, and is now steeped in legend and lore. Today, the history of the end of the war is a matter of great debate and concern in Japan, and sadly the facts are often the first casualty. Even a recent popular film illustrates the problem.

In 1945, Japan was prepared, tough, and would have repelled all invaders. This thesis was part of the political spin present in *Pride: The Fateful Moment*. Something of a phenomenon in 1998, this top-grossing film in Japan beat out *Titanic* and other competitors at the box office. Stirring controversy was good for sales, but the film's well-respected director, Shunya Ito, claimed that his film did not have a political agenda. Focusing on the war crimes trial of former Japanese Prime Minister Hideki Tojo, *Pride: The Fateful Moment* offered a different look at wartime Japan. At least it was different from the point of view of most Westerners who saw the film.

To the victors of World War II, Tojo was the evil face of Japan. Throughout the war, Hollywood propagandists had been especially effective in comparing rather than contrasting Tojo to Hitler and Mussolini. This was never an accurate portrait, but Hollywood's image of the Japanese Hitler died hard. Tojo was found guilty at his postwar trial for having plotted the early offensives of World War II and encouraging the deaths of millions of people across the Asian/Pacific region. Fifty years later, Ito's film stressed and exaggerated the Tojo defense team's arguments at the trial. Complete with flashbacks to both the public and private lives of its subject, *Pride: The Fateful Moment* echoed an old wartime view.[1] Japan, this film argued, had been a victim of Western imperialism. In other words, during World War II Japan was defending itself against the racist world of European and American colonials. The war crimes trials were a sham of victor's justice and revenge, and Prime Minister Tojo was an honorable man caught up in momentous times.

The Americans, according to this film, had it all wrong. Japan was not on the brink of collapse and national suicide in the summer of 1945. The stalwart personality of Hideki Tojo proved the point. Ready to defend his country against all comers, Tojo predicted a Japanese victory should the Americans invade. Any invasion would have condemned the Americans to a higher casualty count than their leaders were ready to accept. The will and determination of the Japanese people, Tojo concluded, would have prevailed over American war weariness anytime. But this was the movie version of Tojo. In real life, Tojo had been the ex-prime minister at the time when Japan feared invasion. He did not, as this film implies, enjoy national recognition as the dedicated symbol of resistance to the American attackers.

Both the screen's Tojo (played by veteran actor Masahiko Tsugawa) and the real Tojo had no apologies for supporting a fight to the death against the European and American colonials. This was not lost on the observant 1990s press. When heavily criticized by some Japanese newspapers (and especially by foreign journalists from Taiwan and the Republic of Korea) as "resurrected wartime propagandists," the cast and crew of *Pride: The Fateful Moment* rallied to the defense of their work. Most said that they simply admired Tojo's courage and dignity, trying to avoid touchy discussions about Japan's wartime mission and destined victory over the almost invasion. But dodging controversy was not in the interest of these filmmakers, and thousands flocked to the movie to see what the fuss was all about. The Japanese press even polled exiting audiences, and their findings were always page one news.

Pride's majority viewer was of the wartime generation, but they were usually accompanied by younger, curious family mem-

torians. Today, as the "greatest generation" passes on, examining how hundreds of thousands of them might have died much earlier during OLYMPIC or CORONET takes on new meaning and significance. And in Japan, there is a new hunger for the truth and the rest of the story. The invasion tale has never deserved to be ignored, and this book must never be the final word.

Notes

1. Objectives, Goals, and the Big Picture

1. Author interview with Tomoko Kamata, housemaid and friend, VOQ Building, Atsugi Naval Air Station, Japan, May 14, 1984. There are plenty of data-filled academic studies on the final air war campaigns against Japan, but two especially readable, memorable, and well-written works include: Kuneta, *City of Fire,* and Kirby, *The War Against Japan.*

2. Kamata interview. A feeling of despair and exhaustion haunted many Japanese at this time. There was even a term for it: a "kyodatsu" condition. It is discussed in general terms in the opening pages of what might soon be recognized as the definitive work on the history of the American postwar occupation of Japan. See John Dower's excellent, ten-years-in-the-making study, *Embracing Defeat.*

3. Kamata interview. For a fascinating study of Yokosuka and its sister bases, see Jackson, *Base of an Empire.*

4. Author interview with George Reeves, editor, *Pacific Stars and Stripes,* and contributing editor, *Asahi Shimbun,* New Sanno Hotel, Tokyo, May 16, 1984.

5. The author, thanks to the assistance of the Kamata family, and the tracking/reconnaissance skills of a former Special Operations Group (SOG) officer, Lt. Joseph Connolly, USN, discovered the first cache of pottery bombs during an expedition through the once-concealed caves of the Ikego base, May 20–21, 1984.

6. Wagstaff, "The 'Suicide Zero' Controversy."

7. This is not a unique view, but it is a primary thesis point of Daniel Okimoto's excellent review of the Japanese economic miracle in the 1980s. Okimoto, *Between MITI and the Market.*

or judge at the Tokyo war crimes trials (1946–1948). He supported most of the defense motions of the indicted war criminals at these trials, and he explains in a clear, no-nonsense fashion his wartime views (and India's) on Japan in this lengthy 1953 work.

11. Hot Springs transcripts, McColm Papers; Armstrong, *Unconditional Surrender,* pp. 15–18.

12. A true consensus in the Filipino political community over "proper" U.S.-Philippines relations concerning the future of Japan was hard to find in 1945. Wurfel, *Filipino Politics,* pp. 8–12; Hot Springs transcripts, McColm Papers.

13. Ibid. (See note 43 below).

14. Zaffra summation, Hot Springs transcripts, McColm Papers.

15. Ibid. (See the Canadian and Australian minutes within the Hot Springs transcripts.) The issues of "exhaustion" and "retreatism" within the ranks of Pacific allies were a matter of concern to Lester J. Foltos in his article "The New Pacific Barrier."

16. Hot Springs transcripts, McColm Papers. Although its lack of detail raises more questions than answers, an adequate general portrait of British bickering and presurrender Allied confusion can be found in Robert E. Ward, "Presurrender Planning: Treatment of the Emperor and Constitutional Changes," in Ward and Yoshikazu, eds., *Democratizing Japan,* pp. 1–41.

17. Hot Springs transcripts, McColm Papers.

18. Ibid.

19. Ibid.

20. Ibid. Wild scenarios over what might or might not happen in post-surrender China were not unusual in top secret U.S. government discussions on China during early 1945. See Iriye and Cohen, *American, Chinese, and Japanese Perspectives,* pp. 243–68.

21. Although Pandit's rhetoric was not welcomed by the White House, her general point of view on "leniency" was essentially the same as the American president's. See Daniels, *White House Witness,* p. 91; Hot Springs transcripts, McColm Papers.

22. Hot Springs transcripts, McColm Papers.

23. Hot Springs transcripts, McColm Papers. Later in 1945, as President Harry Truman wrestled with the A-bomb decision, "certain matters" (including the possibility of a Japanese civil war) were discussed in the White House, but they were not taken as seriously as at Hot Springs. McCloy, *Challenge to American Foreign Policy,* pp. 42–43.

24. Hot Springs transcripts, McColm Papers.

25. Ibid. There is an entire genre of "how the Emperor was saved"

articles, books, and film documentaries on both sides of the Pacific. The Hot Springs argument, i.e. the Emperor as key to postwar peace and quiet, is a common theme within many of them. For a summary, see chapter 2 of Maga, *Judgment at Tokyo*

26. Hot Springs transcripts, McColm Papers. The concern over POWs, wrapped up in the confusion of early postsurrender Japan, is neatly noted in Digman, *Ghost of War,* pp. 100–122.

27. Hot Springs transcripts, McColm Papers. The reasoning expressed at Hot Springs behind the Home Guard concept equals that of later Japanese politicians during the creation of the postwar Japan Self-Defense Force (JSDF). See: Ienaga, *The Pacific War,* p. 246.

28. Hot Springs transcripts, McColm Papers. For more on the French government's position on the Japanese surrender, see the French government–published *Japon 1945. Recueil de documents publie par le gouvernement francais,* vol. 1 (Paris: Alfred Costes, Imprimerie Nationale, 1947). In North America, an original copy of the latter is available in the special collections of McGill University, Montreal, Quebec.

29. Hot Springs transcripts, McColm Papers. Britain's championing of "unity" and "determination" was stirring rhetoric indeed; however, this approach also kept Churchill's Conservative government, and the later Labour government as well, away from specifics, details, and serious planning concerning postwar Japan. Hence, the Hot Springs position soon became the expressed view of British politicians, and this can be seen in the official correspondence and memos on British Japan policy. See the British government–published *Documents on Foreign Policy, Japan,* series D, vol. 11 (London: H.M. Stationary Office, 1961).

30. Hot Springs transcripts, McColm Papers.

31. Ibid.

32. McColm interview.

33. MacArthur and Nimitz to the Joint Chiefs of Staff, JCS 1331/1, April 30, 1945, Sec. 1–B, Entry 421, Box 434 of RG 165, NARA.

34. McColm notes to the "Civil Affairs Handbook–Japan, Section 7: Agriculture," April 1945, Box 28/MHDC of Misc. Hist. Doc. #698–4, Papers of George L. McColm, Truman Library.

35. Ibid. There were few English-language sources on Japan's farming crisis and related political problems during the invasion planning days. To a large degree, the sources issue has not improved. One of best fact-filled yet readable accounts remains Ryoichii Ishi's 1937 work, *Population Pressure and Economic Life in Japan.*

36. McColm notes to the "Civil Affairs Handbook–Japan, Section

1945, all in Box 3/Historical Reports and Research Notes, George M. Elsey Papers, Truman Library.

12. The 1945 Meyer to Truman correspondence on Japan-related issues fills an entire file. His missive of August 11, 1945, to Truman sums up (albeit at great length) Meyer's Japan position quite well. Box 685/OF 197–Misc., 1945–46, Papers of Harry S. Truman, Official File, Truman Library.

13. Truman to Meyer, August 11, 1945, Box 685/OF 197–Misc., 1945–46, Papers of Harry S. Truman, Official File, Truman Library.

14. Niebuhr to Truman, June 25, 1945; John Bennett and (petition co-signers of "A Statement on Our Policy Toward Japan") to Truman, plus June 1945 copies of *Christianity and Crisis,* June 25, 1945, all in Box 685/OF 197–Misc., 1945–46, Papers of Harry S. Truman, Official File, Truman Library.

15. Bishop Peabody to Truman, July 6, 1945, and William Hassett, Secretary to the President, to Peabody, July 11, 1945, all in Box 685/OF 197–Misc., 1945–46, Papers of Harry S. Truman, Official File, Truman Library.

16. Niebuhr to Truman, June 25, 1945, Box 685/OF 197–Misc., 1945–46, Papers of Harry S. Truman, Official File, Truman Library.

17. Hassett to Peabody (and collaborative Hassett/Truman drafts of the same), July 11, 1945, Box 685/OF 197–Misc., 1945–46, Papers of Harry S. Truman, Official File, Truman Library.

4. No Last Ditch Peace Feeler

1. Hoover to Truman, June 7, 1945, Box 685/OF 197–Hoover, 1945–46, Papers of Harry S. Truman, Official File, Truman Library.

2. Tim Maga, "The Evil President: Democrats, Hoover, and the Politics of Image," Symposium on the Foreign Policy of President Herbert Hoover, Herbert Hoover Presidential Library, West Branch, Iowa, September 16, 1999.

3. Ibid.

4. Hoover to Truman, and report, "Memorandum On Ending the Japanese War," June 9, 1945, Box 685/OF 197–Hoover, 1945–46, Papers of Harry S. Truman, Official File, Truman Library.

5. Ibid.

6. Ibid.

7. Ibid.

8. Stimson to Truman, June 14, 1945, Box 685/OF 197–Hoover, 1945–46, Papers of Harry S. Truman, Official File, Truman Library.

9. Truman to Fred Vinson, Executive Director, Office of War Mo-

bilization and Reconversion, June 7, 1945, Box 685/OF 197–Hoover, 1945–46, Papers of Harry S. Truman, Official File, Truman Library.

10. Grew to Truman, and report of the Hoover response group, "Analysis of Memorandum Presented by Mr. Hoover," June 13, 1945, Box 685/OF 197–Hoover, 1945–46, Papers of Harry S. Truman, Official File, Truman Library.

11. Ibid.

12. Ibid.

13. Elsey interview.

14. Ibid. American historians of Japan's occupation period, ranging from Gordon Prange to John Dower, have all commented on Truman's making of Japan policy. A fine collection of statements by postwar academe and from Truman himself can be found in the "Truman and Japan" file of the Justin Williams, Sr. Papers in the Gordon Prange Collection of the University of Maryland Library in College Park, Maryland. Justin was the chief of the legislative division (renamed parliamentary and political division in 1948) of the government section in the occupation government from 1946 to 1952. One of his roles involved surveying U.S. and Truman administration opinion on Japanese politics, and his Papers are dedicated to "mutual understanding" between the United States and Japan.

15. Elsey interview.

16. Charles G. ("Charlie") Ross, Press Secretary, to Truman, and "Memorandum for the President: Unconditional Surrender," June 5, 1945, Box 695/OF 197–Misc., 1945–46, Papers of Harry S. Truman, Official File, Truman Library.

17. "Truman and Japan: 1945–46," Justin Williams Papers, Prange Collection, University of Maryland.

18. Byrnes, *Speaking Frankly*, pp. 224–25. Byrnes served as secretary of state in the Truman administration from 1945 until 1947.

19. Wilson Brown to Elsey, and report, "Defeating Japan," July 1, 1945, Box 1/Japan, Papers of William Rigdon, Assistant Naval Aide to the President, 1942–53, Truman Library.

20. Elsey to Truman, April 16, 1945, and Secretary of State Edward Stettinius to Truman, April 16, 1945, both in Box 159/Subject File: "Policy Manual," President's Secretary's File, Truman Library; Elsey interview.

21. Elsey interview.

22. Nash to Truman, and report, "Peace Without Japan's Unconditional Surrender," June 9, 1945, Box 695/OF 197–Misc., 1945–46, Papers of Harry S. Truman, Official File, Truman Library.

23. Ibid.

France, pp. 50–71; Gottschalk, "Our Vichy Fumble,", pp. 47–56; Leahy, *I Was There,* pp. 386–95; William D. Leahy, "My Position on Japan," speech before the Wisconsin Foreign Affairs Council, undated (probably on or near July 4, 1946), Box 1, Papers of Admiral William D. Leahy, State Historical Society of Wisconsin, Madison, Wisconsin.

39. Elsey interview.

40. Ibid.; June 18 minutes, Department of State, *Foreign Relations of the United States,* pp. 909–11; Leahy, *I Was There,* p. 395.

41. "Losing the Way," an NBC News *Dateline* television special, Brian Williams reporting, August 17, 1999; Tom Brokaw, *The Greatest Generation* (New York: Random House, 1998).

42. Healy to author, September 4, 1999.

5. Japan Stands Alone

1. "Japanese Reaction to the German Defeat," Intercepted Communications, April 14–May 21, 1945, Pacific Strategic Intelligence Section, Commander-In-Chief United States Fleet and Chief of Naval Operations, RG-27, SRH 075, MacArthur Archives. This is a fascinating and extensive day-by-day and sometimes hour-to-hour record of intercepted Japanese messages that were decoded, translated, compiled, bound, and organized under a precise, specific heading for the president's and OSS director's "eyes only." Their declassifications run from the 1980s to the present. For general background on Japan's secret diplomacy, see Seth, *Secret Servants;* Holmes, *Double-Edged Secrets;* Brooks, *Behind Japan's Surrender.*

2. Ibid.

3. Ibid.

4. Ibid.

5. Seminar on German-Japanese Relations, Harvard University, May 1995.

6. "Japanese Reaction to the German Defeat" communiqués.

7. Ibid.; Ben Bruce Blakeney, counsel for the defense, "Petition in the Case of Togo Sigenori," November 19, 1948, RG-41, Box 4/5, "Occupation of Japan, Far East War Trials, December 3, 1945–November 18, 1948," MacArthur Archives.

8. "Russo-Japanese Relations," Intercepted Communications, July 13–August 2, 1945, Pacific Strategic Intelligence Section, Commander-In-Chief United States Fleet and Chief of Naval Operations, RG-27, SRH 085 and SRH 086, MacArthur Archives.

9. "Japanese Reaction to the German Defeat" communiqués.

10. Ibid.

11. Ibid.

12. "Japanese Relations with the Remaining 'Listening Posts' in Europe," Intercepted Communications, May 1–August 1, 1945, Pacific Strategic Intelligence Section, Commander-In-Chief United States Fleet and Chief of Naval Operations, RG-27, SRH-096, MacArthur Archives.

13. Ibid.

14. Ibid.; after the war, Togo, with his former war crimes defense counsel (Ben Bruce Blakeney) acting as ghost writer, published a book that largely rehashed his defense posture during the trials, i.e. that his diplomacy was marked by its innovations and commitment to peace. See Togo, *The Cause of Japan.*

15. "Russo-Japanese Relations" communiqués (see especially PSIS 400–22 here).

16. Ibid.

17. Ibid.

18. Ibid. (see especially H-196632–H-196795 here).

19. Ibid.

20. Maga, *Judgment at Tokyo,* p. 169.

6. Plan Versus Plan

1. MacArthur to Investigative Task Force #15, May 12, 1945, and July 26, 1945, RG-44a, Box 5/24, "Kamikaze Pilots," MacArthur Archives.

2. Ibid.; Appleman, et al., *Okinawa,* pp. 488–90.

3. "#15 Report: Spiritual Intoxication of the Kamikaze," July 26, 1945, RG-44a, Box 5/24, "Kamikaze Pilots," MacArthur Archives. #15 reports were also summarized and analyzed (for the record) several months later by MacArthur's occupation government in Japan. See "Interview with Five Kamikaze," April 1, 1946, RG-44a, Box 5/24, "Kamikaze Pilots," MacArthur Archives. There are a significant number of postwar studies on the kamikaze, but perhaps the most fascinating project involves the 1991 audio book version of Hatsuho Naito's 1981 publication, *Thunder God.* In this audio book, several kamikaze veterans detail their experiences.

4. "#15 Report: Spiritual Intoxication of the Kamikaze," July 26, 1945, RG-44a, Box 5/24, "Kamikaze Pilots," MacArthur Archives; "Interview with Five Kamikaze," April 1, 1946, RG-44a, Box 5/24, "Kamikaze Pilots," MacArthur Archives.

5. See the introduction to the little-known Japanese National Institute for Defense Studies, ed., *Official Military History,* vol. 57,

7. The A-Bomb Debate

1. Woolf, "The Truman Song."

2. Ibid.; "How Your Soldier Goes Across America."

3. Davis, "Operation Olympic."

4. Woolf, "The Truman Song."

5. The Truman Library maintains an up-to-date "Atomic Bomb Decision" file of relevant issues, debates, and articles, including press clippings about "The Taniguchi Issue." This A-bomb file is a combination finding aid and general history compiled by a coalition of Truman Library archivists and graduate students who long sought better organization of A-bomb materials at the library. The file also includes key documentation on the decision to drop the bomb from the Official File, Map Room File, and President's Personal File also at the Truman Library. Some of this material has been made available at the Truman Library Internet webpage for interested researchers. While *Asahi Shimbun, Nikei Weekly,* and *The Japan Times* have covered "Taniguchi Issue" matters well, one of the better straight-to-the-point accounts can be found in Schmetzer, "Survivor of A-Bomb."

6. Schmetzer, "Survivor of A-Bomb."

7. See "The Taniguchi Issue" press clippings subfile discussed in note 5 above.

8. Ibid. Casualty figures vary from study to study, but some of the better analyses of the atomic bomb decision question and examine those figures. See Sherwin, *A World Destroyed;* Sigal, *Fighting to the Finish;* Huber, *Pastel;* and Schoenberger, *Decision of Destiny.*

9. Stewart, "Survivor Story."

10. Alperovitz, *The Decision to Use the Bomb;* Walker, *Prompt and Utter Destruction;* Weintraub, *The Last Great War.*

11. Bernstein, "The Perils and Politics of Surrender."

12. "Minutes of Conference Between Representatives of CINCPAC and CINCAFPAC at Guam, July 21, 1945," RG-38, Box 1/2: "Conference Reports, Oct. '44–Aug. '45," MacArthur Archives; Munson interview; Office of the Military Secretary to Truman, memo, "Relations Between the U.S.S.R. and Japan Since March 1945," July 26, 1945, RG-38, Box 1/2: "Conference Reports, Oct '44–Aug. '45," MacArthur Archives; Elsey interview; Butow; Butow, *Japan's Decision to Surrender,* pp. 70–71; Iriye, *Power and Culture,* pp. 179–80; Leahy, *I Was There,* pp. 258–59.

13. Although he was personally involved in the A-bomb decision, one of the most concise, very readable, and moment-to-moment ac-

counts of the end of the war with Japan remains Stimson, "The Decision to Use the Atomic Bomb."

14. The A-bomb debate is now on-line. In fact, one of the best sources anywhere for the litany of both major and minor points in that debate is: http://www.doug-long.com/index.htm, and the H-DIPLO website: http://h-net2.msu.edu/~diplo/balp.htm. These huge websites serve as sounding boards for historians arguing the facts over the A-bomb decision, and much of the discussion stresses lengthy point-by-point analyses of historian Gar Alperowitz's exhaustive 1995 work, *The Decision to Use the Bomb.*

15. For U.S. public opinion and international opinion about the bomb, see the excellent work by *New York Times* reporter Hanson Baldwin, *Great Mistakes of the War.*

16. For U.S.-U.S.S.R. wrangling over Japan, see the work of Cold War–Far East specialist Odd Arne Wested. Indeed, a special Nobel Committee–sponsored seminar was once held to examine controversial Cold War issues. The role of the A-bomb decision in 1945 Washington-Moscow relations was one of those topics. See Wested, *Reviewing the Cold War.* For a consideration of how Cold War matters influenced the historical study of U.S. foreign policy, see Healy, *The Imperialist Urge,* and Kolko, *Century of War: Politics, Conflicts, and Society.*

17. McCullogh, *Truman,* p. 442. In the late 1990s, the Central Intelligence Agency's Center for the Study of Intelligence and Harvard University's program for Studies of Intelligence Policy joined forces to examine the latest declassified information on the Japan invasion as well as A-bomb decision issues. Examining minute-to-minute decision-making at Potsdam was the major focus of this study's sixth chapter in MacEachin, *Final Months,* pp. 29–31 (narrative) and attached documentation (documents 17 and 18A through F, no page numbers noted on these documents).

18. MacEachin, *Final Months,* pp. 29–30.

19. Merrill, ed., *The Documentary History of the Truman Presidency,* pp. 106–10.

20. McCullogh, *Truman,* p. 442.

21. MacEachin, *Final Months,* pp. 30–31 (and documents 18A through F).

22. Elsey interview.

23. Bernstein, "The Atomic Bombing Reconsidered."

24. "He's Steady Under Fire."

Books, Articles, Videos, and Internet Web Pages

A&E Television and Jack Perkins. *The Propaganda Wars: Japan, the U.S., and the Battle for Hearts and Minds.* New York: A&E film documentary, 1994.

"A-Bomb Debate" Internet Websites: http://www.doug-long.com/index.htm; http://h-net2.msu.edu/~diplo/balp.htm.

Allen, Thomas B., and Norman Polmar. *Codename Downfall: The Secret Plan to Invade Japan.* New York: Simon and Schuster, 1995.

Alperovitz, Gar. *The Decision to Use the Bomb and the Architecture of an American Myth.* New York: Alfred A. Knopf, 1995.

Andrew, Christopher. *For the President's Eyes Only.* New York: Harper Perennial, 1996.

Appleman, Ray E., et al. *Okinawa: The Last Battle.* Washington, D.C.: GPO, 1948.

Armstrong, Anne. *Unconditional Surrender: The Impact of the Casablanca Policy upon World War II.* New Brunswick, N.J.: Rutgers Univ. Press, 1961.

Arnold, Henry H. *Global Mission.* New York: Harper, 1949.

Baldwin, Hanson. *Great Mistakes of the War.* New York: Harper, 1949.

"Ban on Hirohito and Unconditional Surrender Demanded by Senator Lucas," *Peoria Journal Star,* June 4, 1945, p. 1.

Bernstein, Barton J. "The Atomic Bombing Reconsidered." In *Taking Sides: Clashing Views on Controversial Issues in American History Since 1945,* Edited by Larry Maddaras. New York: McGraw-Hill/Dushkin, 2001, pp. 13–24.

——— "The Perils and Politics of Surrender: Ending the War with Japan and Avoiding a Third Atomic Bomb," *Pacific Historical Review* 46, no. 1 (1977), pp. 1–27.

Brooks, Lester. *Behind Japan's Surrender.* New York: McGraw-Hill, 1968.

Butow, Robert C. *Japan's Decision to Surrender.* Stanford, Calif.: Stanford Univ. Press, 1954.

Byrnes, James. *Speaking Frankly.* New York: Harper, 1947.

Cline, Ray S. *Washington Command Post: The Operations Division.* Washington, D.C.: GPO, 1951.

Cohen, Theodore, and Herbert Passin. *Remaking Japan: The American Occupation as New Deal.* New York: The Free Press, 1987.

"Controversial Tojo Film Debuts," *The Japan Times Weekly International Edition,* June 1–7, 1998, p. 4.

Coox, Alvin D. *Japan: The Final Agony.* New York: Ballantine, 1970.

Craven, Wesley Frank, and James L. Cate, eds. *The Air Forces in World War II*. Vol. 5. *The Pacific: Matterhorn to Nagasaki, June 1944 to August 1945*. Chicago: Univ. of Chicago Press, 1955.

Crowell, Todd, and Suvendrini Kakuchi. "Tojo Retold," *Asiaweek* 24, no. 23 (June 12, 1998), pp. 32–33, 38.

Daniels, Jonathan. *White House Witness, 1942–45*. New York: Doubleday, 1975.

Davis, Frank. "Operation Olympic: The Invasion of Japan: November 1, 1945," *Strategy and Tactics* 45 (July/August 1974): pp. 4–20.

Department of the Army, Office of the Chief of Military History. *Homeland Operations Record, Japanese Monograph No. 17*. Washington, D.C.: GPO, October 1945.

Department of State. *Foreign Relations of the United States. Diplomatic Papers: The Conference of Berlin (Potsdam), 1945*. Vol. 1. Washington, D.C.: GPO, 1960.

Digman, Roger. *Ghost of War: The Sinking of the* Awa maru *and Japanese-American Relations, 1945–1995*. Annapolis, Md.: Naval Institute Press, 1997.

Dower, John. *Embracing Defeat: Japan in the Wake of World War II*. New York: Norton, 1999.

———. *Japan in War and Peace*. New York: New Press, 1993.

———. *War Without Mercy: Race and Power in the Pacific War*. New York: Pantheon, 1986.

Drea, Edward J. "Previews of Hell." *MHQ: The Quarterly Journal of Military History* 7 (spring 1995): p. 81.

Elsey, George M. "Some White House Recollections." *Diplomatic History* 12 (summer 1988): pp. 357–64.

———. Transcripts of Oral History Interview with George M. Elsey. Interview by William D. Stilley and Jerald L. Hill, William Jewell College, March 17, 1976. Truman Library Oral History Transcript #398. Transcribed from tapes in July 1985 by the Truman Library Staff. Harry S. Truman Library, Independence, Missouri.

Feis, Herbert. *The China Tangle: The American Effort in China from Pearl Harbor to the Marshall Mission*. Princeton, N.J.: Princeton Univ. Press, 1953.

Foltos, Lester J. "The New Pacific Barrier: America's Search for Security in the Pacific, 1945–1947." *Diplomatic History* 13 (1989): pp. 317–42.

Francillon, Rene J. *Japanese Aircraft of the Pacific War*. London: Putnam, 1970.

Fujiwara, Akira. "The Tojo Fascination." *Boston Globe,* June 9, 1998, p. A02.

Gaddis, John Lewis. "The Emerging Post-Revisionist Synthesis on the

Mikesh, Robert C. *"Kikka."* Washington, D.C.: Monogram Aviation Publications, 1979.

Millis, Walter, ed. *The Forrestal Diaries.* New York: The Viking Press, 1951.

Munson, Brig. Gen. Frederick P. "Oral Reminiscences of Brigadier General Frederick P. Munson." Interview by D. Clayton James, Washington, D.C., July 1971. RG-49, Box 6, "James Interviews," Archives of the General Douglas MacArthur Memorial, Norfolk, Virginia.

Naito, Hatsuho. *Thunder Gods: The Kamikaze Pilots Tell Their Story.* Tokyo: Kodansha/Blackstone Audiobooks, 1991.

Okimoto, Daniel. *Between MITI and the Market.* Stanford, Calif.: Stanford Univ. Press, 1989.

Pal, Radhabinod. *International Military Tribunal for the Far East. Dissentient Judgment.* Calcutta: Sanyal and Co., 1953.

Paxton, Robert O. *Vichy France: Old Guard and New Order, 1940–1944.* New York: Alfred A. Knopf, 1972.

Reeves, George. Interview by author. New Sanno Hotel, Tokyo, May 16, 1984.

Schmetzer, Uli. "Survivor of A-Bomb Urges Japan to Pay Medical Bills," *The Chicago Tribune,* March 2, 2001, p. 4.

Schoenberger, Walter S. *Decision of Destiny.* Athens, Ohio: Ohio Univ. Press, 1969.

Seth, Ronald. *Secret Servants: History of Japanese Espionage.* Westport, Conn.: Greenwood, 1975.

Shaplen, Robert, and Allen J. Fagans. "GIs Around the World Lapped Up the Jap Offer." *Newsweek* 26, no. 8 (August 20, 1945), p. 21.

Sherwin, Martin J. *A World Destroyed: The Atomic Bomb and the Grand Alliance.* New York: Alfred A. Knopf, 1975.

Sigal, Leon V. *Fighting to the Finish: The Politics of War Termination in the United States and Japan, 1945.* Ithaca, N.Y.: Cornell Univ. Press, 1988.

Skates, John Ray. *The Invasion of Japan.* Columbia, S.C.: Univ. of South Carolina Press, 1994.

Stewart, Al. "Survivor Story: Sumiteru Taniguchi." *Daybreak USA* (USA Radio Network interview and broadcast). March 19, 2001.

Stimson, Henry. "The Decision to Use the Atomic Bomb." *Harper's* 194 (February 1947), pp. 97–107.

Swing, Raymond. "What Really Happened at Yalta." *The New York Times Magazine,* February 20, 1949, pp. 10–15.

Troy, Thomas. *Donovan of the CIA: A History of the Establishment of the Central Intelligence Agency.* New York: Acacia Press, 1984.

————. *Wild Bill and Intrepid: Donovan, Stephenson, and the Origins of the CIA.* New Haven: Yale Univ. Press, 1996.

Togo, Shigenori. *The Cause of Japan.* New York: Simon and Schuster, 1956.

Ugaki, Matome. *Fading Victory: The Diary of Admiral Matome Ugaki, 1941–1945.* Pittsburgh: Univ. of Pittsburgh Press, 1991.

U.S. Strategic Bombing Survey. *Japan's Struggle to End the War.* Washington, D.C.: GPO, 1946.

Wagstaff, S.Sgt. Todd, USAF. "The 'Suicide Zero' Controversy." *FEN* [Far East Network] *Television News,* AFRTS (Armed Forces Radio and Television Service broadcast report), Misawa Air Base, Japan, May 16, 1984 (University of Maryland, Asian Division video archives library, Yokota Air Base, Japan).

Walker, Samuel J. *Prompt and Utter Destruction: Truman and the Use of the Atomic Bomb Against Japan.* Chapel Hill: Univ. of North Carolina Press, 1997.

Ward, Robert E., and Sakamoto Yosikazu, eds. *Democratizing Japan: The Allied Occupation.* Honolulu: Univ. of Hawaii Press, 1987.

Weigley, Russell F. *The American Way of War: A History of United States Strategy and Policy.* Bloomington: Indiana Univ. Press, 1977.

Weintraub, Stanley. *The Last Great War: The End of World War II: July-August 1945.* New York: Penguin, 1996.

Wested, Odd Arne. *Reviewing the Cold War: Approaches, Interpretations, Theory.* London: Frank Cass, 2000.

Williams, Brian. "Losing the Way." *NBC News Dateline Special* (NBC network broadcast), August 17, 1999.

Woolf, Dorothy. "The Truman Song." *Newsweek* 26, no. 8 (August 20, 1945), p. 8.

Wurfel, David. *Filipino Politics: Development and Decay.* Ithaca, N.Y.: Cornell Univ. Press, 1988.

Zacharias, Ellis M. "Eighteen Words That Bagged Japan." *Readers Digest* 47 (December 1945), pp. 93–98.

————. "Eighteen Words That Bagged Japan." *Saturday Evening Post* 218 (November 17, 1945), pp. 17, 117–20.

————. "Nippon's Five Secret Peace Bids." *United Nations World.* 3 (August 1949), pp. 25–29.